# Contents

**Photo credits:** Vince Serbin, 6, 7, 8, 10, 11, 12, 14, 15, 18, 20, 28, 32 (bottom), 33 (bottom), 38, 39, 114, 115, 118, 119, 122 (bottom); Beverly Streeter, 32 (top), 33 (upper left), 42, 47, 116, 124; Gordon W. Sousa, Jr., 17, 48; Evelyn M. Shafer, 33 (upper right), 40; Louise Van der Meid, 5; Anne Roslin-Williams, 120, 121; Three Lions, 29.

Mr. Serbin's photos were made through the cooperation of Driftwood Kennels, Bayville, NJ; Highland Kennels, Howell, NJ; Cedarhill Kennel, Freehold, NJ; and Mrs. Alfred Larsen, Seaside Heights, NJ.

**ISBN 0-87666-689-6**

**t.f.h.**

Distributed in the UNITED STATES by T.F.H. Publications, Inc., 211 West Sylvania Avenue, Neptune City, NJ 07753; in CANADA by H & L Pet Supplies Inc., 27 Kingston Crescent, Kitchener, Ontario N2B 2T6; Rolf C. Hagen Ltd., 3225 Sartelon Street, Montreal 382 Quebec; in ENGLAND by T.F.H. (Great Britain) Ltd., 11 Ormside Way, Holmethorpe Industrial Estate, Redhill, Surrey RH1 2PX; in AUSTRALIA AND THE SOUTH PACIFIC by T.F.H. (Australia) Pty. Ltd., Box 149, Brookvale 2100 N.S.W., Australia; in NEW ZEALAND by Ross Haines & Son, Ltd., 18 Monmouth Street, Grey Lynn, Auckland 2 New Zealand; in SINGAPORE AND MALAYSIA by MPH Distributors Pte., 71-77 Stamford Road, Singapore 0617; in the PHILIPPINES by Bio-Research, 5 Lippay Street, San Lorenzo Village, Makati, Rizal; in SOUTH AFRICA by Multipet Pty. Ltd., 30 Turners Avenue, Durban 4001. Published by T.F.H. Publications Inc., Ltd., the British Crown Colony of Hong Kong.

# LABRADOR RETRIEVERS

## by DIANE McCARTY

(1) In a practice session for water retrieval, a pair of black Labs looks shoreward waiting for the training dummy or decoy to be hurled by their handler. This attitude of expectancy is the mark of a good field dog. (2) In retrieval training a number of different decoys are used. This Lab fetches a plastic dummy from the water. (3) A Lab makes his water entry from a dock. His love of water makes the Labrador an enjoyable summertime companion at the beach or backyard pool as well as in the field.

2

3

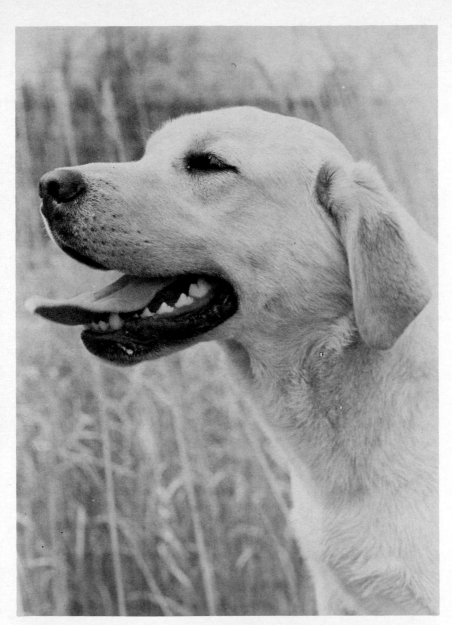

The same hardiness and natural proficiency in water that attracted Newfoundland fishermen in the past to the Labrador Retriever has also made it a favorite among modern day sportsmen. And they have found that this breed's retrieving instincts are just as sharp over ground as in water.

# 1. ORIGINS

The Labrador Retriever, first among the sporting breeds, and regularly within the top five in overall popularity according to American Kennel Club registrations, seems to combine the best of all possible canine sporting worlds for the hunter. He is fast, both in water and over ground, his short double coat offering little resistance in water, thus enabling his swiftness in that milieu. His sense of smell is reputedly without parallel, allowing him to sniff out game through the densest ground cover. He is a good worker by himself, together with others of his breed, or coupled with pointing breeds, for which he makes a good teammate because he willingly seeks out wounded game whereas the pointer will not initiate any follow-up action after the shot has been fired.

In the early days of the breed, the equivalent of today's Labrador was generally lumped together with the Newfoundland and another larger breed of dog then known as the Labrador. Many accounts garnered from various sources generally point to our modern Lab as having sprung from an older breed known as the St. John's Newfoundland. The Labrador Retriever, in fact, did not come from Labrador, but from Newfoundland, though it is not known exactly how he came to be there. The dog began to gain recognition in other countries after he first became noticed in England. It is thought that he first reached English shores, brought there by fisherman who were bringing cod from Newfoundland, supposedly to Dorset. Descriptions of the breed at that time claim its members had webbed feet (an adaptation to their lengthy maritime existence), a short hard coat and an otter tail. This description of the tail is still in current use in the AKC official standard for the breed. Like many of today's modern breeds, the circumstances of his origins and how development to the present day specimen occurred are not exactly known. But one explanation has it that the breed was evolved by Newfoundland fishermen to help them search out sea wrecks and survivors.

Major Maurice Portal, writing in a volume entitled *Guns at Home and Abroad*, says the St. John's dog, probable ancestor of today's Lab, was most likely developed by the fishermen of Newfoundland who "wanted a good strong water dog, since they are reported to have found them useful in cases of wrecks and wreckage on that coast, and crossed the heavy-coated, strong, black Newfoundland retriever with a black Pointer, and evolved in time a hard, short-coated dog with great staying powers..." "That this is probably the origin," continues the Major, "is borne out by the fact that if Labradors are inbred, the result is often a light-made dog, long on the leg, light of bone, with a thin tail and Pointer-like ears."

1

2

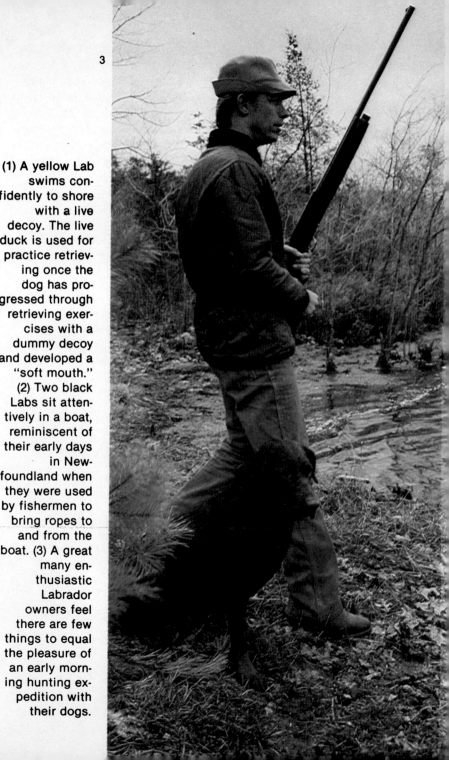

3

(1) A yellow Lab swims confidently to shore with a live decoy. The live duck is used for practice retrieving once the dog has progressed through retrieving exercises with a dummy decoy and developed a "soft mouth." (2) Two black Labs sit attentively in a boat, reminiscent of their early days in Newfoundland when they were used by fishermen to bring ropes to and from the boat. (3) A great many enthusiastic Labrador owners feel there are few things to equal the pleasure of an early morning hunting expedition with their dogs.

Though at least four breeds of dog were generally credited with being Newfoundland dogs, there were discrepancies of character, structure and abilities among these so that one distinguished as St. John's Newfoundland is felt to most closely resemble today's Labrador Retriever. A well-known sportsman of the 1800's, Colonel Peter Hawker, set down a description of two of the breeds in 1814 in a classic piece of writing. The one breed which he denotes as the St. John's Breed closely describes the modern day Lab in his instincts and uses, as well as in his physical aspects. The breed which he calls the "proper Labrador" was very large and strong of limb, with rough hair, small head and a tail which he car-

One of the most highly prized characteristics endearing this breed to sportsmen is its undaunted determination to bag its quarry no matter what the circumstances of terrain or conditions of climate it must contend with.

ried very high. He was valued for his immense strength because his primary use was in pulling sledges loaded with wood to the seashore from inland points. The other smaller breed more closely resembled a pointer in size. He has a long head and nose, fine legs and a deep chest. But where the other had rough hair, this one is characterized by short or smooth hair like today's Lab, and held his tail, unlike the other, not curled over his back. Perhaps most notable in Hawker's decription, because it links the older breed of dog to the newer, is that he wrote of the dog as being "very quick and active in running, swimming or fighting . . . "

Hawker goes on to give further characterization of this dog that agrees in two essential points with the most desirable factors of today's dogs. It also agrees with other sportsmen of his day in their writing about this smaller breed of Newfoundland as opposed to the other large breeds from approximately the same area. According to Hawker, the St. John's breed had no equal for his sense of smell nor for his ability to search out wounded game no matter what the terrain or conditions of undergrowth he must find his way through.

What impressed Hawker about the dog also impressed a contemporary writing some years later. In his book, *The Dog*, written in 1846, Youatt discussed the Newfoundland dogs which he said were used primarily as retrievers. He referred in particular to the St. John's breed, saying this breed was smaller and had the greatest powers of scent. He lauds these dogs for their flexibility in the field saying they were able to work with the pointing breeds, not encroaching upon their area of endeavor. He particularly points up the dog's willingness to look up wounded game and persistence in tracking it down no matter how many or how great the obstacles encountered.

Interestingly enough, Hawker's characterization of the dog, including his tractability and swiftness as well as his powers of scent, is quoted many times in modern writings about the Labrador Retriever where the purpose of the writing is to define the dog and set him apart from other retrieving breeds. The national breed club for this dog saw fit to quote Hawker in the American Kennel Club's official publication which carries the standard for each breed recognized by the AKC.

## THE LABRADOR IN ENGLAND

Around the 1820's the breed was brought to England by the second Earl of Marlmesbury who saw the dog on his native turf. During the following years, the second and third Earls of Marlmesbury carried on breeding programs with this particular strain of retriever and it is believed that the St. John's breed was kept comparatively pure through

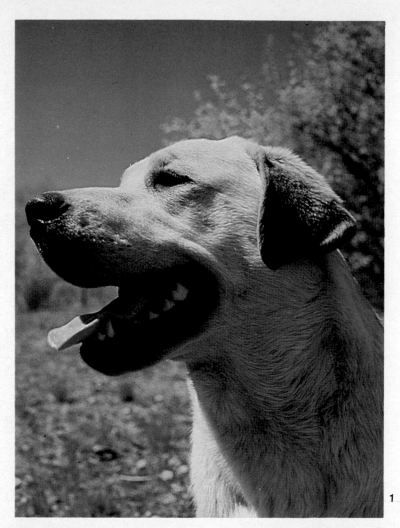

1

(1) The degree of "yellowness" present in the coat of the yellow Lab may vary from one individual dog to another, but the shade must be even throughout, except for gradations of color on ears, underparts, or beneath the tail. This dog shows the desirable dark pigmentation of eyes, eye rims and nose. (2) Because of their short hair, Labs require a minimum of grooming, but field dogs may get muddy or their hair tangled with dirt and brush. (3) Once you have bathed your Lab, be sure he is dried thoroughly. (4) Brushing after a bath gives your dog a well-finished appearance.

2

3

4

their efforts. A letter written by the Earl in the latter 1800's is said to give evidence to the fact that the breed was pure because it contained the statement that he had only bred from dogs which he had first imported from Newfoundland. Unfortunately, not all Labradors being produced at the time were as pure as the dogs of the Marlmesburys. Two factors were responsible for this: in England, not all the breeders were as particular as they were, and secondly, the Labrador, including the St. John's breed, died out because of a heavy tax imposed upon the dogs and certain quarantine laws at the time. This stopped importation of the original dogs and it is thought that breeders began to recreate the breed by outcrossings to setters and pointers. Finally, in an attempt to purify the breed once again, a standard was written up. The Dukes of Buccleuch, avid admirers and breeders of the Labrador in Scotland, kept accurate records of their activities. Through these records it was possible to trace the lineage of the breed, most original stock of which was secured from the Marlmesbury dogs. Two dogs in particular, whose ancestry was traceable largely because of the efforts of Buccleuch, are credited with having been the foundation stock of the modern Labrador Retriever. These were A.C. Butter's Peter of Faskally and Major Portal's Flapper. The English Kennel Club finally gave official recognition to the breed in 1903.

Some 13 years later a Labrador Club was formed in England with Countess Lorna Howe acting as secretary. An ardent fancier of the Labrador breed all her life, Lady Howe owned many outstanding individuals of the breed at her Banchory Kennels, including many winners of the prestigious Crufts show. She had the reputation for knowing and owning fine dogs though she was not a very active breeder.

## THE LABRADOR IN AMERICA

The Countess' dogs were also a great influence in giving this breed its start in America. The Hon. Frank Lord was a leading proponent of the breed in this country. Both his column in the American Kennel Gazette, when the American Kennel Club was an infant organization, and his dogs served to educate retriever enthusiasts in this country to the history as well as the reality of the Labrador.

Mr. Lord was a close friend of Lady Howe from whom he acquired many of the dogs that figured prominently in establishing the breed in America. These dogs included Boli of Blake, first American Bench Champion, whose dam, Banchory Trace, was one of Lady Howe's dogs bred in England. Mr. Lord later brought Banchory Trace to America. Among other dogs owned by Mr. Lord at the time was another one carrying Lady Howe's kennel prefix, Banchory Student.

Mr. Lord frequently visited England, both to observe that country's conformation shows and field trials and in general, to keep up with the trends and progress of the breed among some of that country's leading breeders and kennel owners. After one such trip abroad Mr. Lord commented in his column on a comparison between the English method of showing dogs and the American. He said Labradors there seemed to be more "keen and were shown on a loose lead, rather than held up by the head and tail on a block the way they are shown in this country."

In that column he expressed the wish that American judges go to England and see what a real Labrador looked like as he feared Americans were getting away from correct type. "Above all," said Mr. Lord, "they are shortcoupled with an otter tail!"

Many persons were responsible for the proper growth of the breed in its early days in this country. A great deal of credit goes to the trainers of these first dogs, who were also frequently closely involved with the breeding. Other individuals responsible for giving the breed a substantial forward momentum included J. F. Carlisle and the Hon. W. Averill Har-

The national frisbee finalist of 1978, Thunderbolts Thumper, belonging to Gordon W. Sousa, Jr., Bridgewater, N.J. shows that a Lab's retrieving instincts are not limited to fowl and other game found afield. Retrieving a frisbee "on the wing" is a natural extension of a well-bred Lab's normal love of fetching and chasing.

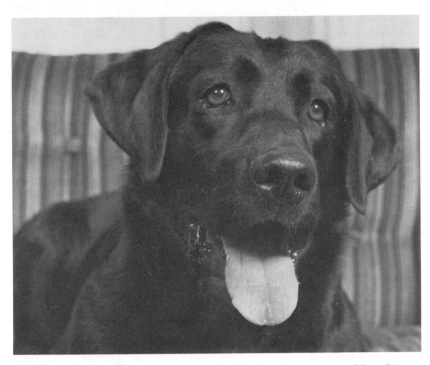

In the early days of the breed, the black Labrador was considered to be most exemplary of the breed type, though yellows and chocolates were to be found almost as early as blacks.

riman whose Arden Kennels became famous for their quality stock. Mr. Carlisle became a cornerstone of the breed in America not only for the prominent quality of dogs he kept at stud, but also because of his avid participation at field trials and shows. Among his dogs, as among those of many leading domestic breeders in the early days of the Lab, can be seen the Banchory prefix of Lady Howe. Mr. Carlisle's imported dogs include Banchory Nightlight, Liddly Bulfinch and Drinkstone Peg among others. Drinkstone Peg also contributed a well-known British-bred American-whelped litter by Dual Champion Bramshaw Bob.

Largely because of the type of input offered by such dogs and the knowledge of these early breeders, American Labs were following in the footsteps of their British cousins toward becoming the leading retriever breed. The origins of the breed in America were well-served because they were not bred for commercial interests, but by people who were avid dog fanciers and interested in the purity of the breed in its functional aspects. They wanted a dog that could perform well in the field. To this extent structure was important, and conformation shows were useful to continually point up the best in structure, coat and tail, all of which were strictly useful to this field dog.

The Arden Kennels of the Hon. W. Averill Harriman with the help of Dr. Samuel Milbank became a powerful molding force in establishing a line of quality dogs in the country. With the importation of his foundation bitch, Peggy of Shipton, and that of the Scottish-bred Raffles of Earlsmoor by Dr. Milbank, a line of dogs developed whose names kept those kennels prominent both at shows and field trials.

Shortly after the Labrador Club was organized, it held the first American field trial for retrievers in 1931. Three of 11 dogs that started actually placed. One of these was one of Mr. Harriman's early Labs, Sam of Arden. The other two dogs that placed were Moose and Glenmere Monarch. Sam had been whelped two years earlier out of Peggy of Shipton. Two years later, that same bitch whelped a litter that produced two field trial champions, Decoy and Blind of Arden. These two not only became prominent in their own right, but were to mold future generations as well.

Interest in field trials developed in this country before interest in the conformation shows became appreciable. Unfortunately, interest groups polarized around either those dogs bred primarily for field work, with the emphasis in these breeding programs on speed or around those dogs bred primarily for conformation shows where the main interest was in appearance and structure, neglecting temperament and the instincts essential to a good field dog. The field dogs, overbred in the direction of a few narrow capabilities tended to become high-strung, while the show dogs, bred with little concern for their field work inheritance, had little interest or inclination to do the work of their more active brothers. Intense competition developed in both fields; professionals began to appear in each.

The majority of good Labs, however, were still kept by people who were primarily interested in keeping the breed pure. These fanciers still retained a highter interest in the smaller variety of trials and shows designed to point up the best qualities of the dog in both areas of endeavor. These were also the owners who actively hunted with their dogs as a pastime and kept them as pets so the original purpose and best interests of the dog were served.

The Labrador Club saw the dangers to the breed inherent in this polarized approach. To preserve hunting interest in the breed, it incorporated a ruling in the standard stating that a dog with an AKC championship could not use the title until he had passed a working test. The English had realized the judiciousness of this ruling years before the breed had become established in this country.

The Labrador has largely escaped much of the commercialism and occasional ruination that can afflict popular breeds when compelled to meet increasing demands of a growing market. Though a polarization between show and field dogs has occurred in the breed's not-too-distant past, its purity and soundness have remained largely intact because of breeders interested in its functional aspects.

# 2. BREED STANDARD

The Labrador Retriever is one breed that has undergone relatively few radical changes by way of outcrossing to distinctly different breeds or outcrossing to distinctly different strains within the breed in order to develop different characteristics. It has been fortunate in the fairly high degree of purity retained in this breed by early fishermen, and later by avid sportsmen interested primarily in the dog as a creature with a specific function to fulfill. To this end, the classes of people with whom the breed has been most closely associated, from the early Newfoundland fishermen to those who took an interest in it as it first gained prominence, have judiciously bred for a dog that physically and temperamentally could best perform under the specific circumstances they imposed upon it.

In the St. John's dog, the one generally accepted as the closest forerunner to our present-day Labrador, the fishermen among whom the dog was first discovered wanted a rugged dog that could withstand and cut through icy water quickly to fetch and carry ropes and nets to and from the boats. They needed a dog whose coat could shed water and ice so its health would not be impaired. The shape and size of the tail which acted as a rudder was another important feature of this dog. Aside from a generally compact structure capable of much endurance, the coat and tail of the original dog remained important as he made the transition to a sporting dog used to retrieve game. His compact body was much suited to his role as game retriever. So there was no reason, as interest in the breed spread and he was used in varying capacities, to change these features, except to perfect the basic material already there. Attention was paid to the head as breeders became aware of a proper length and width of jaw to facilitate carrying fowl and other game. A level bite, though usually always part of the standard of any breed, was particularly important in the case of a retriever so game would not be unduly mangled or destroyed before it reached the hunter.

The Labrador is a relatively modern breed by comparison with many, certain toy and hound breeds among them, that date their close forebearers back to antiquity. This dog began attracting prominent interest as a retriever in the 1800's, if the St. John's Breed is to be taken as its closest ancestor. Several types of retrieving and water dogs were known prior to emergence of the St. John's Breed as a distinct type. In the early days of classifying these dogs, most water retrievers were grouped together and included flat-coats, curly coats, and the variations of Labrador discussed in the last chapter. "Standards" existed at a very early time, albeit not as specific as today's official standard for the breed, because no organized clubs as such had been formed. In these early standards, elements were present that align very closely with certain points found in today's British and American standards for the Labrador.

A book written in 1621 by Gervase Markham contains a "standard" of sorts which foreshadows modern retriever breeds in its description of water dogs of that time. Many of the elements contained in it remain much intact in today's standard. Among other things in Markham's description, he points out that the hair of a water dog "be . . . not loose and shagged," for this type of hair would make the "sport grievous," the ears should be "broad and hanging," his shoulders should be broad, his forelegs straight, his "thighs brawny," his "hocks crooked," and his feet spacious, full and rounded. Similar points from today's standard read: "the coat should be short without wave, the ears should hang . . . close to the head, the legs must be straight from the shoulder to ground and the feet compact, with toes well-arched and pads well-developed; the hocks should be well-bent, strong and muscular in the hindquarters."

Following is an early standard for the Labrador Retriever, believed to be the first ever drawn up.

| | | | |
|---|---|---|---|
| Skull | 15 | Quarter and Stifles | 10 |
| Nose and Jaws | 5 | Legs, Knees and Hocks | 10 |
| Ears and Eyes | 5 | Feet | 5 |
| Neck | 5 | Tail | 5 |
| Shoulders and Chest | 10 | Coat | 5 |
| Loins and Back | 10 | Colour | 5 |
| Symmetry | 5 | Temperament | 5 |

| | |
|---|---|
| The Skull | is wide, but not so much as in the larger variety; flat at top; moderately long. |
| Nose and Jaws | These must be long enough to carry a hare and wide enough for development of the nasal organs of scent; with open nostrils. Teeth level. |
| Ears and Eyes | The ears are small and pendant, close to the head; the hair short with a very light fringe at edge. Eyes of medium size, intelligent and soft. |
| Neck | Moderately long, that is to say, as long as can be got, imported and pure Labradors being often too short to stoop for a scent without diffficulty. |
| Shoulders and Chest | The chest is apt to be barrel-like, but it is better somewhat narrow and deep, for lodging more |

| | |
|---|---|
| | oblique shoulders, and rendering the dog better able to stoop. The back and loins should be strong and well coupled, with deep back ribs. |
| Quarters and Stifles.... | Bent stifles are seldom met in this breed, but they should not be confined in width. The quarters are generally straight, but a slight slope is by no means a disadvantage. |
| Legs, Knees and Hocks. | These ought always to be straight, muscular and strong in bone. The feet are large, and should be specially attended to, as they are apt to be flat and thin-soled. |
| Tail ............... | The tail is bushy without setter feather. It is carried high during excitement but should not be curled over the back. |
| Coat .............. | is moderately short, but wavy, from its length, too great for absolute smoothness. It is glossy and close, admitting wet with difficulty to the skin, owing to its oiliness, but possessing no undercoat. |
| Colour ............. | a rich jet black without rustiness. No quantity of white is admissible, but the best-bred puppies often have a white star. |
| Symmetry........... | is of some importance, as indicating adaption to the work this dog has to do. It is often considerable. |
| Temperament ....... | Without a good disposition and temper, no dog can be made into a good Retriever, and therefore this point should be carefully examined in it. |

The section on the tail in this early standard reflects the outcrosses to setters that were going on at the time. Later emphasis is on the otter tail but both standards remark on its lack of feathering and spirited carriage, while both point out that it is not to be carried curled over the back.

In the statement on color, it is seen that the yellow and chocolate Lab known today had not yet emerged. This did not happen until later and the impression was that even after the emergence of the yellow Lab the black was a hardier type. However, it is felt today that this belief has no basis in fact; all colors, when found in overall good dogs, are strong willing workers of admirable endurance.

Following is the current standard, accepted by the American Kennel Club April 9, 1957.

# STANDARD FOR THE LABRADOR RETRIEVER

*General Appearance:* The general appearance of the Labrador should be that of a strongly built, short-coupled, very active dog. He should be fairly wide over the loins, and strong and muscular in the hindquarters. The coat should be close, short, dense and free from feather.

*Head:* The skull should be wide, giving brain room; there should be a slight stop, i.e. the brow should be slightly pronounced, so that the skull is not absolutely in a straight line with the nose. The head should be clean-cut and free from fleshy cheeks. The jaws should be long and powerful and free from snipiness; the nose should be wide and the nostrils well developed. Teeth should be strong and regular, with a level mouth. The ears should hang moderately close to the head, rather far back; should be set somewhat low and not be large and heavy. The eyes should be of a medium size, expressing great intelligence and good temper, and can be brown, yellow or black, but brown or black is preferred.

*Neck and Chest:* The neck should be medium length, powerful and not throaty. The shoulders should be long and sloping. The chest must be of good width and depth, the ribs well sprung and the loins wide and strong, stifles well turned, and the hindquarters well developed and of great power.

*Legs and Feet:* The legs must be straight from the shoulder to ground, and the feet compact with toes well arched, and pads well developed; the hocks should be well bent, and the dog must neither be cowhocked nor be too wide behind; in fact, he must stand and move true all round on legs and feet. Legs should be of medium length, showing good bone and muscle, but not so short as to be out of balance with rest of body. In fact, a dog well balanced in all points is preferable to one with outstanding good qualities and defects.

*Tail:* The tail is a distinctive feature of the breed; it should be very thick towards the base, gradually tapering towards the tip, of medium length, should be free from any feathering, and should be clothed thickly all round with the Labrador's short, thick, dense coat, thus giving the peculiar "rounded" appearance which has been described as the "otter" tail. The tail may be carried gaily but should not curl over the back.

*Coat:* The coat is another very distinctive feature; it should be short, very dense and without wave, and should give a fairly hard feeling to the hand.

*Color:* The colors are black, yellow, or chocolate and are evaluated as follows:

(a) **Blacks:** All black, with a small white spot on chest permissible.

Eyes to be of medium size, expressing intelligence and good temper, preferably brown or hazel, although black or yellow is permissible.

(*b*) **Yellows:** Yellows may vary in color from fox-red to light cream with variations in the shading of the coat on ears, the underparts of the dog, or beneath the tail. A small white spot on chest is permissible. Eye coloring and expression should be the same as that of the blacks, with black or dark brown eye rims. The nose should also be black or dark brown, although "fading" to pink in winter weather is not serious. A "Dudley" nose, (pink without pigmentation) should be penalized.

(*c*) **Chocolates:** Shades ranging from light sedge to chocolate. A small white spot on chest is permissible. Eyes to be light brown to clear yellow. Nose and eye-rim pigmentation dark brown or liver colored. "Fading" to pink in winter weather not serious. "Dudley" nose should be penalized.

*Movement:* Movement should be free and effortless. The forelegs should be strong and true, and correctly placed. Watching a dog move towards one, there should be no signs of elbows being out in front, but neatly held to the body with legs not too close together, and moving straight forward without pacing or weaving. Upon viewing the dog from the rear, one should get the impression that the hind legs, which should be well muscled and not cowhocked, move as nearly parallel as possible, with hocks doing their full share of work and flexing well, thus giving the appearance of power and strength.

*Approximate Weights of Dogs and Bitches in Working Condition:* Dogs—60 to 75 pounds; bitches—55 to 70 pounds.

*Height at Shoulders:* Dogs—22½ inches to 24½ inches; bitches—21½ inches to 23½ inches.

## THE BRITISH STANDARD

The Kennel Club (Great Britain) standard for the Labrador Retriever is essentially the same as the American Kennel Club standard; there are, however, certain differences that are important enough for specific mention. If your dog is of British registry or if you plan to show him in competitions that are under the jurisdiction of the Kennel Club you should especially note the following variances in the requirements (and also obtain a copy of the complete official standard).

*Head:* The jaws should be medium length.

*Size:* Desired height for dogs, 22 to 22½ inches; for bitches, 21½ to 22 inches.

*Faults:* Undershot or overshot mouth; lack of undercoat; bad action; feathering; snipiness on the head; large or heavy ears; cow-hocked; tail curled over back.

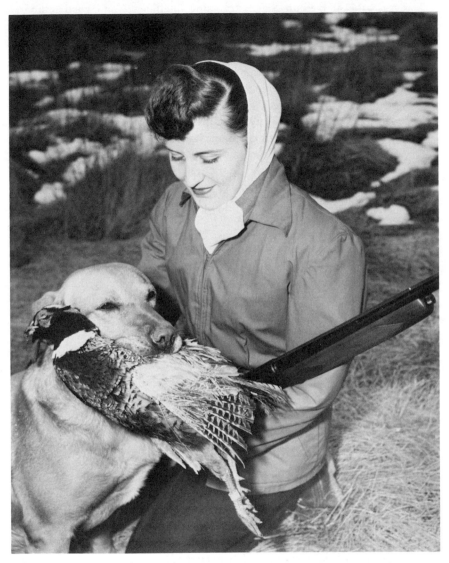

The Labrador's gentle disposition and winsome ways make him a favorite companion on many fronts as well as a much-desired field companion.

# 3. FIELD TRAINING

The most favored retrieving breed, the Labrador is as much of a joy to train as the fully trained dog is to work with in the field, since he is an apt student who learns willingly and with great enthusiasm. The Lab progressively adds to his popularity by extending his skills and field expertise and has in recent years proven himself to be a very capable pinch-hit flushing dog. As with his retrieving abilities, it is also true of his flushing capabilities that the natural talent the dog brings to his work must be honed to its most useful fruition through knowledgeable training. A well-trained dog is a delight, while the poorly trained one gets in both his own and the hunter's way. The well-bred Labrador, however, comes fully equipped with instincts strong enough for his work, and only a light and perceptive touch from a trainer whose mind is in tune with the sensitivity of the breed is needed to mold him into a masterful field dog.

The Labrador is a strong natural swimmer whose particular forte is searching out the difficult fowl that has been downed but only crippled which may elude the hunter indefinitely without the nose of a persistent dog. Used for flushing game, the Lab turns his attention undividedly to marking the fall, going straight to it on command, and making a crisp pick-up, speedy return and faultless delivery.

Some of the equipment used in training the field dog duplicates the usual accessories used in training the pet dog to routine commands. A strong collar and leash are indispensable to keep control of your dog while field training as they are for training the house dog. One essential item for field training is the ordinary police or lifeguard's whistle. This is fitted with a pea-sized cork which allows for a variety of tones and trills when it is blown. It comes closest to effecting the variations of the human voice in giving commands and is, in fact, much more efficient over long distances in the field in getting the dog's attention than the human voice.

Another necessary item is a .22 caliber blank cartridge gun. This is used to accustom the dog during his early training to the sound of a gun being fired, or simply to get him used to abrupt loud noises. Adjustment to loud noises in the field should be made during your dog's preliminary training rather than at a later time when he has supposedly graduated to the finer points of retrieving.

An item many trainers prefer, though it is not absolutely necessary, is a small bell attached to the dog's collar. This enables the trainer to locate the dog in particularly heavy ground cover or to keep track of him on the return from an especially distant retrieve. Though it can be used on your Labrador, it is more favored for pointing breeds and smaller field dogs

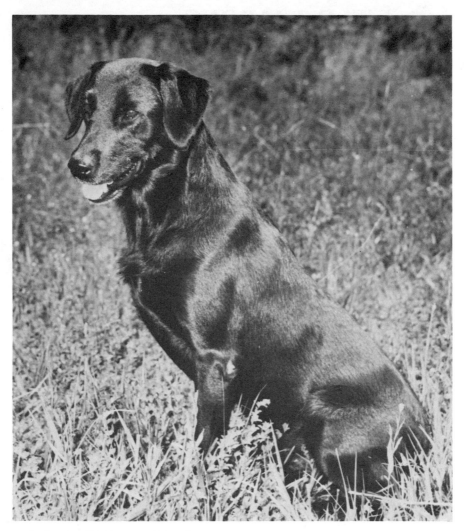

Labrador Retrievers, if bred properly, come fully equipped with retrieving instincts intact. To bring these to the fore they must be trained with a regard for their intelligence and without an overly heavy hand for discipline.

(1) While he waits for a "Go" command, the Labrador remains fully alert. (2) The Lab that is properly trained for the home and field can't help but be a good traveling companion. (3) A dog cannot be useful in the field unless it is under control at all times.

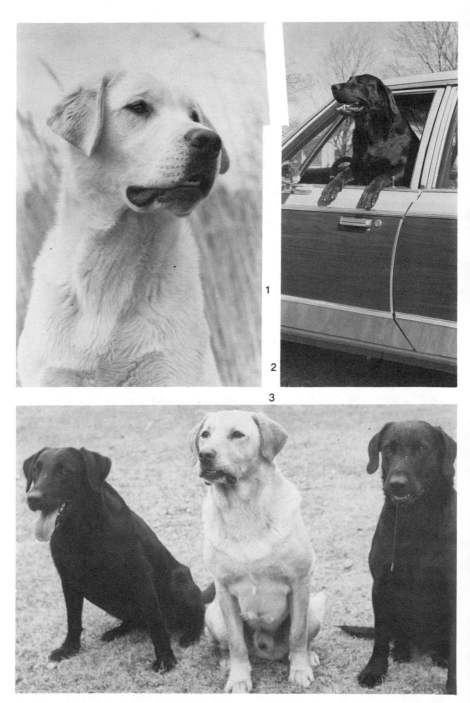

1

2

3

such as Bassets and Beagles. In the latter case, use of the bell is actually a safety factor to protect the smaller dogs from the gunfire of other hunters who may not be aware of their presence because of their small size.

Training scents are commercially manufactured compounds that serve a wide variety of uses. They can be employed to train a dog onto a scent as well as off particular scents of animals not being hunted, but for which the dog may harbor a natural curiosity.

Most important to a fetch dog like the Lab is the training dummy which comes in varying sizes and shapes, and is made of canvas stuffed with shredded foam rubber. It is durable, heavy enough to be thrown a good distance, yet light enough for a dog to easily retrieve. Very buoyant in water, its ruggedness still allows for a good deal of use on land as well.

If your retriever is to double as a flushing dog, two additional tools can be used in training: the check-cord and the flushing whip. The check-cord is used primarily to steady pointing breeds, but it may also be used to dictate and control the range of your Lab when he is used for flushing. It is made of a strong but thin nylon which slips through field grass and brush easily, and is mostly used in 25, 50, 75 and 100 foot lengths.

The flushing whip, as its name indicates, is used to flush out close-lying game birds from tall grass. It is made of harness or latigo leather which for about ⅔ of its 30 inch length is wrapped around a flexible spring and sewn shut. The remainder of that length is left unstitched to form two or more loose strap-like pieces used to flail the grass. Equipped with a leash-type snap fastener, it doubles as a handy short leash for the field as well as a disciplinary tool when such force is called for.

Invaluable to the Lab owner who has gone onto advanced training with his dog is a device called the "Retriev-R-Trainer." This training tool is similar to the beer can launcher known to target shooters. It consists of a hand grip, chamber that holds a blank cartridge and training dummy, and straight rod that serves as a trigger. When pulled straight back, the trigger fires the cartridge at the same time launching the dummy up to a distance of 250 feet, depending on the size of the cartridge and angle at which the device has been fired. It is useful both in teaching the dog to become accustomed to the sound of gunfire and to mark a distant fall.

There are other types of training tools available, but they are mainly used for other types of field dogs and are not strictly applicable to retrievers. It might be well to note here, however, the three different types of training collars available for use in training your dog. The common choke used in routine backyard training of your pet or show dog is also used in training the field dog, and in most cases is quite adequate to get the job done. For dogs that require a bit more persuasion than usual, the prong collar is used. This is the chain link collar fitted with two rows of blunt metal prongs on the inside of the collar. These tighten against the dog's neck only when the collar is tightened. The most severe collar for the very stubborn dog is a leather choke collar that contains a row of small spikes with semi-blunted tips. Like the two collars mentioned above, this one also effects its disciplinary purpose only when the trainer manually tightens it by pulling on the lead. This collar is not designed to be cruel. Attention should be given to the spikes set in the collar; if they are too sharp they should be filed down, but not so far as to cancel out their effectiveness.

Now that you have assembled your equipment, the next thing in line for training your Labrador is to teach him the working vocabulary needed to accomplish his business in the field. But before you actually turn your new puppy loose in the field, there is a lot of training, or just plain "civilizing," that will have ordinarily gone on at home or in the backyard that will contribute greatly to his efficient field performance. Basic to his control in the field are the everyday commands such as "Come," "Sit," "Stay," etc. If he has not learned these by the time you are ready to teach him pertinent commands of field work, you will have a dog that ranges wherever he wants to, interferes with other hunters and their dogs, or just plain is not around when you want him. Control is the key word and this early "civilizing" is an important part of controlling him.

As your Labrador becomes a full-fledged field dog retrieving on command, he will learn to respond to an average working vocabulary of about two dozen words although this can vary with the relative intelligence of the dog and the rapport he has with his master. Older dogs have been known to respond to a much larger vocabulary and in some cases need practically no command at all. They have come to know their masters and the work they are about so well, that they know almost by intuition when to fetch, when not to, and when a particularly elusive quarry has been dropped that requires diligent searching out. However, this sort of familiarity and rapport cannot be immediately expected of the beginner until he becomes a seasoned gun dog. It must be remembered that the fewer commands and the less verbiage used to get across simple ideas, the more quickly he will learn.

Labradors possess two outstanding characteristics of temperament that perhaps lay the foundation for owners to fall into two training errors unless they school themselves to be astute. The owner must train himself to be aware of this breed's high intelligence and gentle and willing disposition which makes him an excellent companion and a wholly satisfactory field and water dog. Such awareness must recognize that the Lab has the learning capacity of a highly intelligent dog but not the intelligence of a human. This combination of personality traits may lead

(1) A preliminary to field training is the routine commands of backyard training. A choke collar may enhance this. (2) The Lab, once fully trained, knows when to enter the water and does so with verve and style. (3) Learning the "Lie Down" command with hand signals is an important step to learning the hand signals used in the field. (4) Whistle training for the field requires putting the Lab through the same paces as with the voice command, but using certain whistle blasts for the verbal command. (5) The Lab's expression is marked by alertness and serenity.

1

2

3

4

5

the understandably prejudiced Lab owner into giving commands in a conversational way resembling the way one human would communicate to another. Communicating with the dog in short monosyllabic words is designed to get the dog's attention. Longer words may fail precisely because there is no sharp distinct sound the dog can associate with the action expected of him.

Use of the same word to indicate the same action is a difficult discipline to impose on oneself as it is not a natural method of communication for humans. We tend to use different words or expressions to say the same thing to one another when a direction has to be given more than once, but this results in confusion for the field dog. When the dog is to fetch, then "Fetch" is the word to use for that action each time that action is to be initiated. To tell your dog to "go get it and bring it on in here" one time, "round it up" another time, and "let's get it up here" still another time, is to ultimately create confusion for your dog. The dog is to get one meaning from all of these commands: bring the dead bird here. The briefest, catchiest sounding word for the command, "Fetch," is the best. To make him wade through a maze of different terms and expressions which his experience does not enable him to interpret is to greatly slow down the entire learning process. Though hunting dogs have a great deal of flexibility and your Lab would eventually grasp what you wanted from him, such conversational commands would ultimately dull his keen capacities of understanding, and tax both his vast desire to learn and your patience. By the time your conversational commands have been peppered with a few choice oaths because he is not catching on, the whole process has been lengthened even more.

The key to his learning what is expected of him is to demonstrate what the word means over and over again until it is learned. For this purpose, the trimmer the vocabulary, the faster the dog learns. Though he will necessarily have to add more words to his vocabulary as he matures into a full-fledged field dog (especially if he is used to flush as well as retrieve), the rule still holds true. If the same words can be used for a variety of functions, the better it is. Going back to his "civilizing" stages, the word "No" can be used when he is on the couch where he does not belong, it can be used to order him from a room where he is not welcome, it can be used to keep him from chasing the family cat, and so on. Although other words can be used for each of these orders also, why clutter up the dog's vocabulary when use of the same word to accomplish the same purpose in each case is not only effective, but reinforces the meaning of that word? Such vocabulary trimming and application of one command to several different orders is that much more effective in the trained gun dog. For although his vocabulary has been shortened, this is not true of his understanding of the command or his adherence to it. In fact, you have undoubtedly speeded up his obedience of your command by not requiring him to wade through extraneous verbiage.

Another reason for a trim vocabulary is that it can easily be transferred into a system of whistle signals. It is obvious in this instance that the fewer word commands your dog has to master, the less difficult it will be to assign a distinctive whistle signal for each, since any whistle has much less flexibility for intonation and different sounds than does the human voice. While a vast number of outdoorsmen use a combination of voice commands and visual directions to summon and guide their dogs, a great many use the whistle coupled with these same visual signals. Use of the whistle has a number of advantages, the most obvious being that it saves one's voice and throat, both of which sustain a great deal of wear and tear after a full day's hunting in field and stream. Secondly, a whistle is much more clearly heard over a longer distance than is the human voice, and can penetrate to places where the dog has ranged even when the eye cannot see him. Thirdly, the whistle described earlier has enough flexibility that, with a short efficient vocabulary, there is no trouble in devising a distinct whistle blast or combination of whistle sounds for each command. The crisp, definitive sound of the whistle is authoritative and commands immediate attention and respect.

It happens that retrievers especially are intimately bound up in the audio-visual system used by hunters in field and wood to direct their dogs. This is especially true of unmarked falls. The retriever must rely upon his owner to give him a "line" on the felled bird and to direct him thereafter whether to "Stop" or go to the "Left," "Right," "Back," or "Forward." In fact, it is this interlocking teamwork between hunter and dog, each relying on the other to do his part in finally getting the bird bagged, that is part and parcel to a satisfying hunting experience. If the bird has only been crippled, the system is particularly important to the dog in retrieving it, wasting the least possible amount of time searching it out. But without the visual system coupled with the audio, the dog would have to use a ripple effect system of locating the game, particularly with unmarked falls. The time consumed in this method, plus the haphazard approach, would result in frustration and reduced quota for the hunters, and would ultimately lessen the enjoyment both dog and man experience on these excursions.

In teaching the dog to respond to the signals, there are basically three different whistle signals he must learn, and four, possible five, hand signals. But while these sound like very few, as with your common backyard commands, they must be learned through constant repetition and demonstration. Patience is the key word here, on the part of the trainer. The most useful and well-trained dog must have confidence to proceed on his own instincts and trust in a trainer which comes from not being overly disciplined. The whistle signals consist of 1) teaching the dog to "Stop" or "Whoa" which automatically means to the dog that he will immediately fix his attention on the trainer for further directions; 2) sending the dog on; 3) calling the dog in. Hand signals mainly consist of showing the dog in which direction to search: left, right, back, or forward. The fifth hand signal is a reinforcement, really, to an above-mentioned whistle signal. It consists of extending the arm outward, palm turned toward the dog, and is used to stop the dog at close range or reinforce the stop signal already given on the whistle.

To begin his training, start with the command that is the easiest to learn, the "Go on." Teaching response to voice as well as whistle at the

**The place for gundogs while hunters take aim and fire, is sitting attentively at the heels of their masters, marking the fall, and staying well out of gun range until the command is given to retrieve.**

outset is the easiest way for your dog to learn both forms of audio command. Because he is always eager to be off and "hunting" he will be quick to associate the meaning with the words in this command. Taking him by the collar, give the verbal command to "Go on," releasing his collar as you say it. Immediately after issuing the voice command, blow two short blasts on the whistle in quick succession. Again, because he is eager to be loose, this is one lesson he should learn speedily. The association between whistle and voice command should be motivated by his desire to be loose, so he will shortly grasp the meaning of the whistle when used alone without the voice command.

Teaching your Lab to come at the whistle signal may be a bit more difficult than the first, but no more difficult than teaching him to come on voice command. Besides, he has already had experience in his civilizing stage, so the "Come" command is not new to him. The only new thing he has to contend with in the field is the vastly more exciting surroundings that offer so much more for his curiosity to be drawn to. Use of a check-cord in the beginning will be helpful.

Call the dog to you in the usual way; just after you have given the verbal command, give a long vibrating blow on the whistle. If he does not respond to the voice command, obvious use of the check-cord is indicated. But he should soon get the idea and respond to the whistle whether on or off the check-cord.

Stopping the dog by use of the whistle is undoubtedly the most difficult, and yet this command, too, has had some previous usage in the backyard training to "Sit." Use of the whistle to stop your dog has different vocal equivalents in the different hunting breeds. For the retriever, stopping is the equivalent of the "Sit" command with the addition of the dog's expectation of receiving a further order from the trainer. With the leash on, begin to heel with your dog. Stop and give the order to "Sit." Immediately follow the vocal with a single short blast on the whistle, then pull up on the lead while exerting pressure on his rump to make him sit down. Once he is responding well to the command on lead, switch from the leash to the check-cord. Exercise the command with the check-cord extended to ever more distant lengths until the dog has the idea no matter how far away from you he is. He will soon be obeying the command without any prodding from either leash or check-cord.

The voice and whistle commands must be letter-perfect before going on to the visual part of the lessons, i.e. directional signals using hands and arms. But once he is responding well to the audio commands, then it is time to teach the visual signals. Extending the whole right arm straight in front of you, simply sweep it in the direction in which you want your dog to go. Accompany this with the "Go on" blasts on the whistle. If you

(1) Labradors may be put through their paces using either logs, a training dummy, or a live decoy.

(2) This Lab shows the correct totally attentive, receptive expression while waiting for his master to issue the next command.

(3) Field training for the Lab, as with backyard training, may be begun on a normal length lead, graduating to 25, 50 or 100 foot lengths of nylon cord as the commands he learns become more advanced, until he is finally ready to perform off lead.

want him to go straight ahead no movement of the arm is necessary. Exaggerated arm movement makes for greater visibility to your dog, so if you want him to go to the left, use your left arm sweeping the whole arm in that direction while giving the whistle signal. Likewise for sending him to the right. For the command "Back," your arm is flexed and extended in the direction of the dog, palm toward him, while giving the voice command, "Back." Follow up with the whistle signal.

Many trainers find that rewarding with treats and tidbits speeds up the learning process. As in more normal training, be lavish with praise when your dog has done well. Don't expect a seasoned gun dog out of a first-time beginner. But you will find that after one or two seasons with your young dog and *consistent* usage of the audio-visual signals, the system of communication between you and your Labrador will be quite effective, offering a pleasurable bond that grows with every hunting season. If you are also to use your Lab as a flushing dog, his vocabulary will have to be expanded, but not by much. In essence, what he will have to learn in addition to what you have already taught him in order to be a proficient

**The dog that becomes the masterful field dog is one with which his owner has exercised a great deal of patience, appreciating the dog's full potential.**

retriever, is how to quarter his ground in front and to the sides of the gunner, and at a pace and distance that keeps him within gun range. If he is kept in good control by whistle and voice, he will learn very quickly to establish a good range and quartering pattern.

A good gun dog is one that anticipates the hunt as you do, is tuned into the general activities of the hunt, knows when his job begins practically before you have given him a command. One of the most important factors in developing a good gun dog is to allow him to progress at his own natural pace. Assuming the dog you have is descended from good breeding stock bred especially to keep the hunting instinct of the breed intact, his interest in the hunt will come to the fore naturally. The only thing that will be needed from you, and this through training, is to channel those instincts properly. They cannot be placed there if the dog does not exhibit them naturally. But they can be stultified and inhibited by pushing a young dog too fast, expecting too much from him before he has had experience, exposing him to too much noise and confusion, to too many people giving too many different commands, and by overdisciplining. By pushing him too far too fast, your Labrador will turn into one that retrieves in a mechanical, stiff manner, whose natural interest does not quicken to the sport and one that brings no joy to hunt with.

The wise hunter knows that if he is to realize the full potential of a good dog, he will spend most of that first season his dog is in the field hunting alone with him and exercising much patience. There is no fast way to produce a good retriever, and letting the dog develop at his own pace and find his own methods will pay dividends later.

The new puppy has an adjustment to make. This is the first time he has been alone without littermates and expected to relate to a world made up largely of humans instead of others like himself.

# 4. THE NEW PUPPY

## PREPARING FOR THE LABRADOR PUPPY'S ARRIVAL

In choosing a puppy, be certain beforehand that each member of the family is truly enthusiastic about having this particular breed of dog as an addition to their circle. Dogs are much too intelligent not to sense whether or not they are liked. If your puppy feels unwanted, you may find an unhappy dog on your hands that could easily turn into a "problem child." Before buying, research the breed and make sure it is the one for you. Besides reading, a good way to learn about your prospective pet is to observe one of the same breed in its permanent home surroundings. Most owners will be only too happy to show off their furry friend.

One of the most important factors to consider when selecting a dog, whether it is to be a pet or show dog, is its temperament. When looking at a litter of puppies for a prospective purchase, spend time just quietly observing them. Usually the most outgoing or aggressive puppy is your best bet. However, do not overlook the more reserved puppy. Most dogs are wary of strangers, so reserve may indicate caution, not timidity. He may calmly accept your presence when he senses that all is well. In any event, never force yourself on a puppy—let him come to you. Beware of the puppy that hides in the corner and won't emerge until you have left. Chances are he will always be high-strung and may develop more undesirable habits as a result of his nervousness.

Because at least three out of four prospective purchasers of dogs want to buy a young rather than an adult or almost adult dog, the problem of preparing for the arrival of a permanent canine house guest almost always means preparing for the arrival of a puppy. This is not to say that there is anything wrong with purchasing an adult dog; on the contrary, such a purchase has definite advantages in that it often allows freedom from housebreaking chores and rigorous feeding schedules, and these are a definite benefit to prospective purchasers who have little time to spare. Since the great majority of dog buyers, however, prefer to watch their pet grow from sprawlingly playful puppyhood to dignified maturity, buying a dog, practically speaking, means buying a puppy. Before you get a puppy be sure that you are willing to take the responsibility of training him and caring for his physical needs. His early training is most important, as an adult dog that is a well-behaved member of the family is the end product of your early training. Remember that your new puppy knows only a life of romping with his littermates and the security of being with his mother, and that coming into your home is a new and sometimes frightening experience for him. He will adjust quickly if you are patient with him and show him what you expect of him. If there are small children in the family be sure that they do not abuse him or play roughly with him. A puppy plays hard, but he also requires frequent periods of rest. Before he comes, decide where he is to sleep and where he is to eat. If your puppy does not have a collar, find out the size he requires and buy an inexpensive one, as he will soon outgrow it. Have the proper grooming equipment on hand. Consult the person from whom you bought the puppy as to the proper food for your puppy, and learn the feeding time and amount that he eats a day. Buy him some toys—usually the breeder will give you some particular toy or toys which he has cherished as a puppy to add to his new ones and to make him less homesick. Get everything you need from your pet shop before you bring the puppy home.

## MALE OR FEMALE?

Before buying your puppy you should have made a decision as to whether you want a male or female. Unless you want to breed your pet and raise a litter of puppies, your preference as to the sex of your puppy is strictly a personal choice. On the whole both sexes are pretty much the same in disposition and character, and both make equally good pets.

## SHOW DOG OR PET?

It is well to define in your own mind the purpose for which you want a dog, and to convey this to the breeder. A great deal of disappointment and dissatisfaction can be avoided by a meeting of the minds between seller and buyer.

Although every well-bred healthy member of the breed makes an ideal companion and pet, actual pet stock is usually the least expensive of the purebred registered stock. The person who asks for a pet, pays a pet-geared price for the animal. Pet stock is least expensive because these dogs are deemed unsuitable for breeding or exhibition in comparison to the standard of perfection for the breed. Generally only skilled breeders and judges can point out the structural differences between a pet and show quality dog.

If you are planning to show your dog, make this clear to the breeder and he will aid you in selecting the best possible specimen of the breed. A show quality dog may be more expensive than one meant for a pet, but it will be able to stand up to show ring competition.

## WHERE TO BUY YOUR LABRADOR PUPPY

Once you have decided on the particular breed that you want for your pet, your task is to find that one special dog from among several outlets. Buying a well-bred, healthy dog is your foremost concern. By doing a little research in the various dog magazines and newspapers you can locate the names and addresses of breeders and kennels in your area that are known for breeding quality animals. The American Kennel Club will also furnish you with addresses of people to contact that are knowledgeable about your chosen breed.

Your local pet shop, although necessarily restricted from carrying all breeds in stock, may sometimes be able to supply quality puppies on demand. Due to the exorbitant amount of space and time needed to properly rear puppies, pet shops generally prefer to assist owners by supplying all the tools and equipment needed in the raising and training of the puppies. The pet shop proprietor, if unable to obtain a dog for you, can often refer you to a reputable kennel with which he has done business before.

## SIGNS OF GOOD HEALTH

Picking out a healthy, attractive little fellow to join the family circle is a different matter from picking a show dog: it is also a great deal less complicated. Often the puppy will pick you. If he does, and it is mutual admiration at first sight, he is the best puppy for you. Trust your eyes and hands to tell if the puppy is sound in body and temperament. Ears and eyes should not have suspicious discharges. Legs should have strong bones; bodies should have solid muscles. Coats should be clean. Lift the hair to see that the skin is free of scales and parasites.

Reliable breeders and pet shops will urge you to take your puppy to the veterinarian of your choice to have the puppy's health checked, and will allow you at least two days to have it done. It should be clearly understood whether rejection by a veterinarian for health reasons means that you have the choice of another puppy from that litter or that you get your money back. Be sure to get the details of this policy before you purchase any puppy.

## PAPERS

When you buy a purebred dog you should receive his American Kennel Club registration certificate (or an application form to fill out), a pedigree and a health certificate made out by the breeder's veterinarian. The registration certificate is the official A.K.C. paper. If the puppy was named and registered by his breeder you will want to complete the transfer and send it, with the appropriate fee, to the American Kennel Club. They will transfer the dog to your ownership in their records and send you a new certificate. If you receive, instead, an application for registration, you should fill it out choosing a name for your dog, and mail it, with the fee, to the A.K.C.

The pedigree is a chart showing your puppy's ancestry and is not a part of his official papers. The health certificate will tell what shots have been given and when the next ones are due. Your veterinarian will be appreciative of this information, and will continue with the same series of shots, if they have not been completed. The health certificate will also give the date on which the puppy has been wormed.

## REGISTERING YOUR LABRADOR PUPPY

For information on how to register a new litter of pedigreed dogs owners may write to the following:

**American Kennel Club**
51 Madison Avenue
New York, New York 10010
United States of America

**Canadian Kennel Club**
2150 Bloor Street West
Toronto, Ontario M6S 4V7
Canada

**Australian Kennel Club**
Royal Show Grounds
Ascot Vale, Victoria
Australia

**British Kennel Club**
1 Clarges Street
Picadilly, London W.1
England

## THE PUPPY'S FIRST NIGHT WITH YOU

The puppy's first night at home is likely to be disturbing to the family. Keep in mind that suddenly being away from his mother, brothers and sisters is a new experience for him; he may be confused and frightened. If you have a special room in which you have his bed, be sure that there is nothing there with which he can harm himself. Be sure that all lamp cords are out of his reach and that there is nothing that he can tip or pull over. Check furniture that he might get stuck under or behind and objects that he might chew. If you want him to sleep in your room he probably will be quiet all night, reassured by your presence. If left in a room by himself he will cry and howl, and you will have to steel yourself to be impervious to his whining. After a few nights alone he should adjust. The first night that he is alone it is wise to put a loud-ticking alarm clock, as well as his toys, in the room with him. The alarm clock will make a comforting noise, and he will not feel that he is alone.

## YOUR LABRADOR PUPPY'S BED

Every dog likes to have a place that is his alone. He holds nothing more sacred than his own bed whether it be a rug, dog crate, or dog bed. If you get your puppy a bed be sure to get one which discourages chewing. Also

During the new puppy's first few days and nights with you, he may be quite vocal in letting his feelings of abandonment and loneliness for littermates be known. Approach him with patience, giving him as much company as possible and this period will pass quickly.

be sure that the bed is large enough to be comfortable for him when he is full grown. Locate it away from drafts and radiators. A word might be said here in defense of the crate, which many pet owners think is cruel and confining. Given a choice, a young dog instinctively selects a secure place in which to lounge, rest or sleep. The walls and ceiling of a crate, even a wire one, answer that need. Once he regards his crate as a safe and reassuring place to stay, you will be able to leave him alone in the house.

## FEEDING YOUR PUPPY

At the time of purchase, most breeders will give you food for a few days, along with instructions for feeding so that your puppy will have the same diet he is accustomed to until you can buy a supply at your pet shop.

As a general rule, a puppy from weaning time (six weeks) to three months of age should be fed four meals a day; from three months to six months, three meals; from six months to one year, two meals. After a year, a dog does well on one meal daily. There are as many feeding schedules as there are breeders, and puppies do fine on all of them, so it is best for the new owner to follow the one given him by the breeder of his puppy.

The diet and proportions that are right for your puppy are not necessarily those that would be right for another. Whatever keeps him healthy, active and happy is the proper diet.

## HOUSEBREAKING

While housebreaking your puppy, do not let him have the run of the house. If you do you will find that he will pick out his own bathroom, which may be in your bedroom or in the middle of the living room rug. Keep him confined to a small area where you can watch him, and you will be able to train him much more easily and speedily. A puppy does not want to dirty his bed, but he does need to be taught where he should go. Spread papers over his living quarters, then watch him carefully. When you notice him starting to whimper, sniff the floor or run agitatedly in little circles, rush him to the place that you want to serve as his relief area and gently hold him there until he relieves himself. Then praise him lavishly. When you remove the soiled papers, leave a small damp piece so that the puppy's sense of smell will lead him back there next time. If he makes a mistake, wash the area at once with warm water, followed by a rinse with water and vinegar or sudsy ammonia. This will kill the odor and prevent discoloration. It shouldn't take more than a few days for him to get the idea of using newspapers. When he becomes fairly consistent, reduce the area of paper to a few sheets in a corner. As soon as you think he has the idea fixed in his mind, you can let him roam around the house a bit, but keep an eye on him. It might be best to keep him on a leash the first few days so that you can rush him back to his paper at any signs of an approaching accident.

The normal healthy puppy will want to relieve himself when he wakes up in the morning, after each feeding and after strenuous exercise. During early puppyhood any excitement, such as the return home of a member of the family or the approach of a visitor, may result in floor-wetting, but that phase should pass in a few weeks. Keep in mind that you can't expect too much from your puppy until he is about five months old. Before that, his muscles and digestive system just aren't under his control.

## OUTDOOR HOUSEBREAKING

You can begin outdoor training on a leash even while you are paper-training your puppy. First thing in the morning take him outdoors (to the curb, if you are in the city) and walk him back and forth in a small area until he relieves himself. He will probably make a puddle and then walk around, uncertain of what is expected of him. You can try standing him over a newspaper, which may give him the idea. Praise your dog every time taking him outside brings results, and he will get the idea. You'll find, when you begin the outdoor training, that the male puppy usually requires a longer walk than the female. Both male and female puppies will squat. It isn't until he is older that the male dog will begin to lift his leg. If you hate to give up your sleep, you can train your puppy to go out-doors during the day and use the paper at night.

## ALL DOGS NEED TO CHEW

Puppies and young dogs need something with resistance to chew on while their teeth and jaws are developing—for cutting the puppy teeth, to induce growth of the permanent teeth under the puppy teeth, to assist in getting rid of the puppy teeth at the proper time, to help the permanent teeth through the gums, to assure normal jaw development and tó settle the permanent teeth solidly in the jaws.

The adult dog's desire to chew stems from the instinct for tooth clean-ing, gum massage and jaw exercise—plus the need for an outlet for periodic doggie tensions.

Dental caries as it affects the teeth of humans is virtually unknown in dogs—but tartar accumulates on the teeth of dogs, particularly at the gum line, more rapidly than on the teeth of humans. These accumulations, if not removed, bring irritation, and then infection which erodes the tooth enamel and ultimately destroys the teeth at the roots. Most chewing by adult dogs is an effort to do something about this problem for themselves.

Tooth and jaw development will normally continue until the dog is more than a year old—but sometimes much longer, depending upon the breed, chewing exercise, the rate at which calcium can be utilized and many other factors, known and unknown, which affect the development of individual dogs. Diseases, like distemper for example, may sometimes arrest development of the teeth and jaws, which may resume months, or even years later.

This is why dogs, especially puppies and young dogs, will often destroy property worth hundreds of dollars, when their chewing instinct is not diverted from their owner's possessions, particularly during the widely varying critical period for young dogs.

Saving your possessions from destruction, assuring proper develop-ment of teeth and jaws, providing for 'interim' tooth cleaning and gum massage, and channeling doggie tensions into a non-destructive outlet are, therefore, all dependent upon the dog having something suitable for chewing readily available when his instinct tells him to chew. If your pur-poses, and those of your dog, are to be accomplished, what you provide for chewing must be desirable from the doggie viewpoint, have the necessary functional qualities, and above all, be safe for your dog.

It is very important that dogs not be permitted to chew on anything they can break, or indigestible things from which they can bite sizeable chunks. Sharp pieces, from such as a bone which can be broken by a dog, may pierce the intestine wall and kill. Indigestible things which can be

Nylabone®, a unique 100 percent nylon chew bone, is the perfect chewing pacifier for young dogs in their teething stage, or even for older dogs to help satisfy that occasional urge to chew. Unlike many other dog bones on the market today, Nylabone® does not splinter or fall apart. It will last indefinitely and as it is used it frills, becoming a doggie toothbrush that cleans teeth and massages gums.

bitten off in chunks, such as toys made of rubber compound or cheap plastic, may cause an intestinal stoppage, if not regurgitated—to bring painful death, unless surgery is promptly performed.

Strong natural bones, such as 4 to 8 inch lengths of round shin bone from mature beef—either the kind you can get from your butcher or one of the variety available commercially in pet stores—may serve your dog's teething needs, if his mouth is large enough to handle them effectively.

You may be tempted to give your puppy a smaller bone and he may not be able to break it when you do—but puppies grow rapidly and the power of their jaws constantly increases until maturity. This means that a growing dog may break one of the smaller bones at any time, swallow the pieces and die painfully before you realize what is wrong.

Many people make the mistake of thinking of their dog's teeth in terms of the teeth of the wild carnivores or those of the dog in antiquity. The teeth of the wild carnivorous animals, and the teeth found in the fossils of the dog-like creatures of antiquity, have far thicker and stronger enamel than those of our contemporary dogs.

All hard natural bones are highly abrasive. If your dog is an avid chewer, natural bones may wear away his teeth prematurely; hence, they then should be taken away from your dog when the teething purposes have been served. The badly worn, and usually painful, teeth of many mature dogs can be traced to excessive chewing on natural bones.

Contrary to popular belief, knuckle bones which can be chewed up and swallowed by the dog provide little, if any, useable calcium or other nutriment. They do, however, disturb the digestion of most dogs and cause them to vomit the nourishing food they need.

An old leather shoe is another popular answer to the chewing need—but be very sure that the rubber heel, all nails, and other metal parts such as lace grommets, metal arches, etc., have been removed. Be especially careful to get all of the nails. A chunk of rubber heel can cause an intestinal stoppage. If it has a nail in it, the intestine wall may be pierced or torn. Then there is, of course, always the hazard that your dog may fail to differentiate between his shoe and yours, and eat up a good pair while you're not looking.

Dried rawhide products of various types, shapes, sizes and prices are available on the market and have become quite popular. However, they don't serve the primary chewing functions very well; they are a bit messy when wet from mouthing, and most dogs chew them up rather rapidly—but they have been considered safe for dogs until recently. Now, more and more incidents of death, and near death, by strangulation have been reported to be the result of partially swallowed chunks of rawhide swelling in the throat. More recently, some veterinarians have been attributing cases of acute constipation to large pieces of incompletely digested rawhide in the intestine.

The nylon bones, especially those with natural meat and bone fractions added, are probably the most complete, safe and economical answer to the chewing need. Dogs cannot break them or bite off sizeable chunks; hence, they are completely safe—and being longer lasting than other things offered for the purpose, they are economical.

Hard chewing raises little bristle-like projections on the surface of the nylon bones—to provide effective interim tooth cleaning and vigorous gum massage, much in the same way your tooth brush does it for you. The little projections are raked off and swallowed in the form of thin shavings—but the chemistry of the nylon is such that they break down in the stomach fluids and pass through without effect.

The toughness of the nylon provides the strong chewing resistance needed for important jaw exercise and effective help for the teething functions—but there is no tooth wear because nylon is non-abrasive. Being inert, nylon does not support the growth of microorganisms—and it can be washed in soap and water, or it can be sterilized by boiling or in an autoclave.

Nylabone® is highly recommended by veterinarians as a safe, healthy nylon bone that can't splinter or chip. Instead, Nylabone is frizzled by the dog's chewing action, creating a toothbrush-like surface that cleanses the teeth and massages the gums. Nylabone® and Nylaball®, the only chew products made of flavor-impregnated solid nylon, are available in your local pet shop.

Nothing, however, substitutes for periodic professional attention to your dog's teeth and gums, not any more than your toothbrush can do that for you. Have your dog's teeth cleaned by your veterinarian at least once a year, twice a year is better—and he will be healthier, happier and far more pleasant to live with.

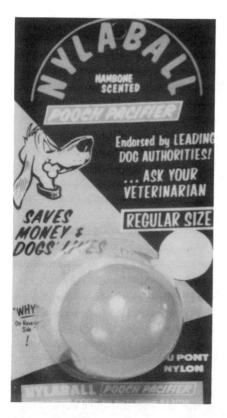

Nylaball®, another fully nylon dog pacifier, is a hygienic chew product that will hold your dog's interest for hours. Impregnated with ham flavor, it is a wholly safe, long-lasting product that cannot endanger your dog's life with the threat of fragments that may become lodged in his throat.

# 5. OBEDIENCE TRAINING

## WHEN TO START TRAINING

You should never begin *serious* obedience training before your dog is seven or eight months old. (Some animal psychologists state that puppies can begin training when seven weeks old, if certain techniques are followed. These techniques, however, are still experimental and should be left to the professional trainer.) While your dog is still in his early puppyhood, concentrate on winning his confidence so he will love and admire you. Basic training can be started at the age of three or four months. He should be taught to walk nicely on a leash, sit and lie down on command, and come when he is called.

## YOUR PART IN TRAINING

You must patiently demonstrate to your dog what each word of command means. Guide him with your hands and the training leash, reassuring him with your voice, through whatever routine you are teaching him. Repeat the word associated with the act. Demonstrate again and again to give the dog a chance to make the connection in his mind.

Once he begins to get the idea, use the word of command without any physical guidance. Drill him. When he makes mistakes, correct him, kindly at first, more severely as his training progresses. Try not to lose your patience or become irritated, and never slap him with your hand or the leash during the training session. Withholding praise or rebuking him will make him feel bad enough.

When he does what you want, praise him lavishly with words and with pats. Don't continually reward with dog candy or treats in training. The dog that gets into the habit of performing for a treat will seldom be fully dependable when he can't smell or see one in the offing. When he carries out a command, even though his performance is slow or sloppy, praise him and he will perform more readily the next time.

## THE TRAINING VOICE

When you start training your dog, use your training voice, giving commands in a firm, clear tone. Once you give a command, persist until it is obeyed, even if you have to pull the dog to obey you. He must learn that training is different from playing, that a command once given must be obeyed no matter what distractions are present. Remember that the tone and pitch of your voice, not loudness, are the qualities that will influence your dog most.

Be consistent in the use of words during training. Confine your commands to as few words as possible and never change them. It is best for only one person to carry on the dog's training, because different people will use different words and tactics that will confuse your dog. The dog who hears "come," "get over here," "hurry up," "here, Rex," and other commands when he is wanted will become totally confused.

## TRAINING LESSONS

Training is hard on the dog and the trainer. A young dog just cannot take more than ten minutes of training at a stretch, so limit the length of your first lessons. Then you can gradually increase the length of time to about thirty minutes. You'll find that you too will tend to become impatient when you stretch out a training lesson. If you find yourself losing your temper, stop and resume the lesson at another time. Before and after each lesson have a play period, but don't play during a training session. Even the youngest dog soon learns that schooling is a serious matter; fun comes afterward.

Don't spend too much time on one phase of training, or the dog will become bored. Always try to end a lesson on a pleasant note. Actually, in nine cases out of ten, if your dog isn't doing what you want it's because you're not getting the idea over to him properly.

## YOUR TRAINING EQUIPMENT AND ITS USE

The leash is more properly called the lead, so we'll use that term here. The best leads for training are the six-foot webbed-cloth leads, usually olive-drab in color, and the six-foot leather lead. Fancier leads are available and may be used if desired.

You'll need a metal-link collar, called a choke chain, consisting of a metal chain with rings on each end. Even though the name may sound frightening, it won't hurt your dog, and it is an absolute MUST in training. There is a right and a wrong way to put the training collar on. It should go around the dog's neck so that you can attach the lead to the ring at the end of the chain which passes over, not under the neck. It is most important that the collar is put on properly so it will tighten when the lead is pulled and ease when you relax your grip.

The correct way to hold the lead is also very important, as the collar should have some slack in it at all times, except when correcting. Holding the loop in your right hand, extend your arm out to the side, even with your shoulder. With your left hand, grasp the lead as close as possible to the collar, without making it tight. The remaining portion of the lead can

Your local pet store is the source of a large selection of leads and collars that can be used for training or showing, or just taking your pet for a walk. Since puppies quickly outgrow their first collars and leads, plan to purchase at least two sets of equipment.

be made into a loop which is held in the right hand. Keep this arm close to your body. Most corrections will be made with the left hand by giving the lead a jerk in the direction you want the dog to go.

## HEELING

"Heeling" in dog language means having your dog walk alongside you on your left side, close to your leg, on lead or off. With patience and effort you can train your dog to walk with you even on a crowded street or in the presence of other dogs.

Now that you have learned the correct way to put on your dog's collar and how to hold the lead, you are ready to start with his first lesson in heeling. Make the dog sit at your left side. Using the dog's name and the command "Heel," start forward on your LEFT foot, giving a tug on the lead to get the dog started. Always use the dog's name first, followed by the command, such as "Rex, heel." Saying his name will help get his attention and will let him know that you are about to give a command.

Walk briskly, with even steps, going around in a large circle, square or straight line. While walking, make sure that your dog stays on the left side and close to your leg. If he lags behind, snap gently on the lead to get him up to you, then praise him lavishly for doing well. If he forges ahead or swings wide, stop and jerk the lead sharply and bring him back to the proper position. Always praise him when he returns to the correct place. As soon as you have snapped the lead to correct your dog, let it go slack again at the desired length. Don't drag the dog or keep the lead taut as this will develop into a tug of war which is ineffective.

To keep your dog's attention, talk to him as you keep him in place. You can also do a series of fast about-turns, giving the lead a jerk as you turn. He will gradually learn that he must pay attention or be jerked to your side. You can vary the routine by changing speeds, doing turns, figure-eights, and by zig-zagging across the training area.

## "HEEL" MEANS "SIT," TOO

To the dog, the command "Heel" will also mean that he has to sit in the heel position at your left side when you stop walking with no additional command from you. As you practice heeling, make him sit whenever you stop, at first using the word "Sit," then with no command at all. He'll soon get the idea and sit down when you stop and wait for the command "Heel" to start walking again.

## TRAINING TO SIT

Training your dog to sit should be fairly easy. Stand him on your left side, holding the lead fairly short, and command him to "Sit." As you give the verbal command, pull up slightly with the lead and push his hindquarters down. Do not let him lie down or stand up. If he does lie down, snap up on the lead until he rises to a sitting position again. If he is slow to respond, tug more sharply until he has done what you want him to. Keep him in a sitting position for a moment, then release the pressure on the lead and praise him. Constantly repeat the command as you hold him in a sitting position, thus fitting the word to the action in his mind. If he moves at all, immediately repeat the command and press him into a sitting position. After a time he will begin to get the idea and will sit without having to push his hindquarters down. When he reaches that stage, insist that he sit on command. Praise him often, always rewarding a correct action with your praise and affection.

# THE "LIE DOWN" OR "DOWN"

The object of this is to get the dog to lie down either on the verbal command "Down" or when you give the hand signal, your hand raised in front of you, palm down. However, until the dog is really sure of the meaning of the command, and will do it by himself with no forcible action from you, the hand signal should only be used to accompany the verbal command. This command may be more difficult at first because it places the dog in a defenseless position, which may cause him to bolt away. Be lavish with your praise and affection when he has assumed the correct position and he will soon learn that nothing bad happens to him, and on the contrary will associate the "Down" position with pleasing his master or mistress.

Don't start training to lie down until the dog is almost letter-perfect in sitting on command. Place the dog in a sit, and kneel before him. With both hands, reach forward to his legs and take one front leg in each hand, thumbs up, holding just above the elbows. Lift his legs slightly off the ground and pull them somewhat out in front of him. Simultaneously, give the command "Down" and lower his front legs to the ground.

Hold the dog down and stroke him to let him know that staying down is what you want him to do. This method is far better than forcing a young dog down. Using force can cause him to become very frightened and he will begin to dislike any training. Always talk to your dog and let him know that you are very pleased with him, and soon you will find that you have a happy working dog.

After he begins to get the idea, slide the lead under your left foot and give the command "Down." At the same time, pull the lead. This will help get the dog down. Meanwhile, raise your hand in the down signal. Don't expect to accomplish all this in one session. Be patient and work with the dog. He'll cooperate if you show him just what you expect him to do.

# THE "STAY"

The next step is to train your dog to stay either in a "Sit" or "Down" position. As before, use the lead to teach this command until your dog is responding perfectly to your instruction, then you may try it off the lead. To begin with the Sit-Stay, place your dog in a sitting position beside you in the automatic heel-sit position. Holding the leash in one hand (most trainers prefer the left), take a long step forward and turn to face him holding your free hand open, palm toward him, fingers pointing downward, in front of his nose and speak the command "Stay." If he offers to follow you, as it would be natural for him to do since this has been his ready position for heel, snap up on the lead to return him to the sit, put your hand in front of his face and repeat the command firmly once more. Allow him to remain sitting for a few seconds before going through the procedure again. Each time he successfully performs, praise him profusely and show him you are pleased with him.

Repeat this procedure until your dog behaves as if he understands what is expected of him. When he has mastered this procedure, step away to the right of him, then behind, then a few steps forward, a few steps to the side, and so on, until you have gone the full length of the leash. Anytime your dog offers to follow you, snap upward on the leash, extending your arm palm forward to him and repeat the command sharply. When he has demonstrated a willingness to remain in the correct position while you walk the full extent of the lead, you are ready to train him to remain in position using a longer length of cord, about 25 or 30 feet, and finally the Sit-Stay off the lead.

Once the Sit-Stay is learned, you can teach the Down-Stay by beginning with the Down command, then apply approximately the same methods as in the Sit-Stay.

## THE COME ON COMMAND

You can train your dog to come when you call him if you begin when he is young. At first, work with him on lead. Sit the dog, then back away the length of the lead and call him, putting into your voice as much coaxing affection as possible. Give an easy tug on the lead to get him started. When he does come, make a big fuss over him—it might help at this point to give him a small piece of dog candy or food as a reward. He should get the idea soon. You can also move away from him the full length of the lead and call to him something like "Rex, come," then run backward a few steps and stop, making him sit directly in front of you.

Don't be too eager to practice coming on command off lead. Wait until you are certain that you have the dog under perfect control before you try calling him when he's free. Once he gets the idea that he can disobey a command and get away with it, your training program will suffer a serious setback. Keep in mind that your dog's life may depend on his immediate response to a command to come when he is called. If he disobeys off lead, put the lead back on and correct him severely with jerks of the lead.

## TEACHING TO COME TO HEEL

The object of this is for you to stand still, say "Heel," and have your dog come right over to you and sit by your left knee in the heel position. If your dog has been trained to sit without command every time you stop, he's ready for this step.

Sit him in front of and facing you and step back one step. Moving only your left foot, pull the dog behind you, then step forward and pull him around until he is in a heel position. You can also have the dog go around by passing the lead behind your back. Use your left heel to straighten him out if he begins to sit behind you or crookedly. This may take a little work, but he will get the idea if you show him just what you want.

## THE STAND

Your dog should be trained to stand in one spot without moving his feet, and he should allow a stranger to run his hand over his body and legs without showing any resentment or fear. Employ the same method you used in training him to stay on the sit and down. While walking, place your left hand out, palm toward his nose, and command him to stay. His first impulse will be to sit, so be prepared to stop him by placing your hand under his body, near his hindquarters, and holding him until he gets the idea that this is different from the command to sit. Praise him for standing, then walk to the end of the lead. Correct him strongly if he starts to move. Have a stranger approach him and run his hands over the dog's back and down his legs. Keep him standing until you come back to him. Walk around him from his left side, come to the heel position, and make sure that he does not sit until you command him to. This is a very valuable exercise. If you plan to show your dog, he will have to learn to stand in a show pose and allow the judge to examine him. The judge will run his hands along the dog's back and down the legs, so it is important that the dog stands calmly and steadfastly.

## TRAINING SCHOOLS AND CLASSES

There are dog training schools in all parts of the country, some sponsored by the local humane society.

If you feel that you lack the time or the skill to train your dog yourself, there are professional dog trainers who will do it for you, but basically dog training is a matter of training YOU and your dog to work together as a team, and if you don't do it yourself you will miss a lot of fun. Don't give up after trying unsuccessfully for a short time. Try a little harder and you and your dog will be able to work things out.

## ADVANCED TRAINING AND OBEDIENCE TRIALS

Once you begin training your dog and you see how well he does, you'll probably be bitten by the "obedience bug"—the desire to enter him in obedience trials held under American Kennel Club auspices.

The A.K.C. obedience trials are divided into three classes: Novice, Open and Utility.

In trials for advanced obedience degrees, your dog will have to successfully accomplish two scent discrimination exercises. From among several objects like the ones above, he will have to choose the one that has been touched by his handler or owner and carries that person's scent.

In the Novice Class the dog will be judged on the following basis:

### TEST MAXIMUM SCORE

| Test | Maximum Score |
|------|--------------|
| Heel on lead | 40 |
| Stand for examination | 30 |
| Heel free—off lead | 40 |
| Recall (come on command) | 30 |
| One-minute sit (handler in ring) | 30 |
| Three-minute down (handler in ring) | 30 |
| Maximum total score | 200 |

If the dog "qualifies" in three shows by earning at least 50% of the points for each test, with a total of at least 170 for the trial, he has earned the Companion Dog degree and the letters C.D. (Companion Dog) are entered after his name in the American Kennel Club records.

The hurdle is used in different events in advanced obedience competition. It figures in the single jump, in the retrieve, and in the directed jump. The bar is adjustable, so that the height a dog must jump to successfully accomplish the particular exercise will be proportional to his size. Informal hurdles can be simulated out of a variety of different items for backyard or indoor practice before the actual trial.

After the dog has earned his Companion Dog title, he is eligible to enter the Open Class competition and compete for his next degree. He will be judged on this basis:

TEST MAXIMUM SCORE

Heel free ............................................... 40
Drop on recall ......................................... 30
Retrieve (wooden dumbbell) on flat ........................ 20
Retrieve over obstacle (hurdle) ............................ 30
Broad jump ............................................. 20
Three-minute sit (handler out of ring) ...................... 30
Five-minute down (handler out of ring) ..................... 30
Maximum total score .................................. 200

Again he must qualify in three shows for the C.D.X. (Companion Dog Excellent) title, earning at least 50% of the points for each test, with a total of at least 170 for the trial. He is then eligible to compete in the Utility Class, where he can earn the Utility Dog (U.D.) degree in these rugged tests:

TEST MAXIMUM SCORE

Scent discrimination (picking up article handled by master
  from group) Article 1 ................................. 30
Scent discrimination Article 2 ............................ 30
Directed Retrieve ....................................... 30
Signal exercise (heeling, etc., on hand signal) ................. 40
Directed jumping (over hurdle and bar jump) ................. 40
Group examination ...................................... 30
Maximum total score .................................. 200

For more complete information about these obedience trials, write for the American Kennel Club's *Regulations and Standards for Obedience Trials*. Dogs that are disqualified from breed shows because of neutering or physical defects are eligible to compete in these trials. Besides the formal A.K.C. obedience trials, there are informal "match" trials in which dogs compete for ribbons and inexpensive trophies. These shows are run by many local fanciers' clubs and by all-breed obedience clubs. In many localities the humane society and other groups conduct their own obedience shows. Your local newspaper, pet shop proprietor or kennel club can keep you informed about such shows in your vicinity, and you will find them listed in the different dog magazines or in the pet column of your paper.

# 6. BREEDING YOUR DOG

## THE QUESTION OF SPAYING

If you feel that you will never want to raise a litter of purebred puppies, and if you do not wish to risk the possibility of an undesirable mating and surplus mongrel puppies inevitably destined for euthanasia at the local pound, you may want to have your female spayed. Spaying is generally best performed after the female has passed her first heat and before her first birthday; this allows the female to attain the normal female characteristics, while still being young enough to avoid the possible complications encountered when an older female is spayed. A spayed female will remain a healthy, lively pet. You often hear that an altered female will become very fat. However, if you cut down on her food intake, she will not gain weight.

On the other hand, if you wish to show your dog in American Kennel Club competition (altered females are disqualified) or enjoy the excitement and feeling of accomplishment of breeding and raising a litter of quality puppies, particularly in your breed and from your pet, then do not spay your dog until a more appropriate time.

Male dogs are almost never altered (castrated) unless they exhibit excessive sexual tendencies.

## SEXUAL PHYSIOLOGY

Females usually reach sexual maturity (indicated by the first heat cycle, or season) at eight or nine months of age, but sexual maturity may occur as early as six months or as late as thirteen months of age. Generally, the larger the breed is the longer it takes to reach full maturity.

The average heat cycle (estrus period) lasts for twenty or twenty-one days, and occurs approximately every six months. For about five days immediately preceeding the heat period, the female generally displays restlessness and an increased appetite. The vulva, or external genitals, begins to swell. The discharge, which is bright red at the onset and gradually becomes pale pink to straw in color, increases in quantity for several days and then slowly subsides, finally ceasing altogether. The vaginal discharge is subject to much variation; in some bitches it is quite heavy, in others it may never appear, and in some it may be so slight as to go unnoticed.

About eight or nine days after the first appearance of the discharge, the female becomes very playful with other dogs, but will not allow a mating

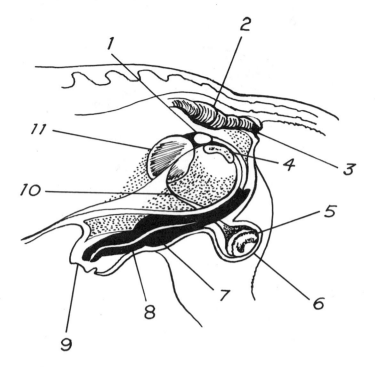

Reproductive system of a male dog: 1. Prostate 2. Rectum 3. Anus 4. Section of pelvic bone 5. Testicle 6. Scrotum 7. Bulb (part of Penis) 8. Penis 9. Sheath 10. Vas deferens 11. Bladder.

to take place. Anywhere from the tenth or eleventh day to the seventeenth or eighteenth day, the female will accept males and be able to conceive. Many biologists apply the term "heat" only to this receptive phase rather than to the whole estrus period, as is commonly done by dog fanciers.

The ova (egg cells) from the female's ovaries are discharged into the oviduct toward the close of the acceptance phase, usually the sixteenth to eighteenth day. From the eighteenth day until the end of the cycle, the female is still attractive to males, but she will repulse their advances. The entire estrus, however, may be quite variable; in some females vaginal bleeding ends and mating begins on the fourth day; in others the discharge may continue throughout the entire cycle and the female will not accept males until the seventeenth day or even later.

The male dog—simply referred to by fanciers as the "dog" or "stud," in contrast to the female, which is referred to as the "bitch"—upon reaching sexual maturity, usually at about six to eight months, is able,

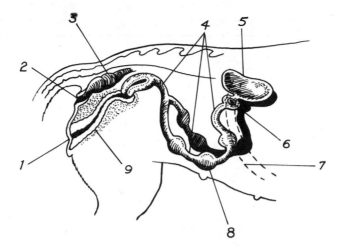

Reproductive system of the bitch: 1. Vulva 2. Anus 3. Rectum 4. Uterus 5. Kidney 6. Ovary 7. Ribs (indicated) 8. Developing embryo 9. Vagina.

like other domesticated mammals, to breed at any time throughout the year.

The testes, the sperm-producing organs of the male, descend from the body cavity into the scrotum at birth. The condition of cryptorchidism refers to the retention of one or both testes within the body cavity. A testicle retained within the body cavity is in an environment too hot for it to function normally. A retained testicle may also become cancerous. If only one testicle descends, the dog is known as a monorchid; if neither descends, the dog is known as an anorchid (dog fanciers, however, refer to a dog with the latter condition as a cryptorchid). A monorchid dog is a fertile animal; an anorchid is sterile.

The male dog's penis has a bulbous enlargement at its base and, in addition, like the penis of a number of other mammals, contains a bone. When mating occurs, pressure on the penis causes a reflex action that fills the bulb with blood, swelling it to five times its normal size within the female. This locks, or ties, the two animals together. After ejaculation, the animals usually remain tied for fifteen to thirty minutes. However, they may separate very quickly or remain together an hour or more, depending on the length of time for the blood to drain from the bulb.

## CARE OF THE FEMALE IN ESTRUS

If you have a dog-proof run within your yard, it will be safe to leave your female in season there; if you don't have such a run, she should be shut indoors. Don't leave her alone outside even for a minute; she should be exercised only on lead. If you want to prevent the neighborhood dogs from congregating around your doorstep, as they inevitably will as soon as they discover that your female is in season, take her some distance from the house before you let her relieve herself. Take her in your car to a park or field for a chance to "stretch" her legs (always on lead, of course). Keep watch for male dogs, and if one approaches take the female back to the car. After the three weeks are up you can let her out as before with no worry that she can have puppies until her next season.

Some owners find it simpler to board their female at a kennel until her season is over. However, it really is not difficult to watch your female at home. There are various products on the market which are useful at this time. Although the female in season keeps herself quite clean, sometimes she unavoidably stains furniture or rugs. You can buy sanitary belts made expecially for dogs at your pet shop. Consult your veterinarian for information on pills to be taken to check odor during this period. There also is a pill that prevents the female from coming in season for extended periods, and there are many different types of liquids, powders and sprays of varying efficiency used to keep male dogs away. However, the

There are several products on the market designed to make life easier for both you and your bitch during the estrus cycle. Sanitary pads for dogs are one of these items and come complete with a belt for holding the pad in place.

one safe rule (whatever products you use) is: keep your bitch away from dogs that could mount her.

## SHOULD YOU BREED YOUR MALE?

Deciding whether or not to use a male dog as a stud is a question with two sides. The arguments for and against using a dog as a stud are often very close to ridiculous. A classic example would be the tale that once you use a dog as a stud he will lose his value as a show dog or any one of the other functions a dog may have. A sound rule may well be: if you have a stud who has proven his worth at the shows, place his services out for hire, if only for the betterment of the breed; if your dog is not of show quality, do not use him as a stud.

Top champion studs can bring their owners many dollars in breeding revenue. If the stud is as good as you feel he is, his services will soon be in great demand. Using a dog as a stud will not lower his value in other functions in any way. Many breeders will permit a male dog to breed an experienced female once, when about a year old, and then they begin to show their stud until he has gained his conformation championship. He is then placed out for hire through advertising in the various bulletins, journals and show catalogues, and through the stud registers maintained by many pet shops and kennel clubs.

## SHOULD YOU BREED YOUR FEMALE?

If you are an amateur and decide to breed your female it would be wise to talk with a breeder and find out all that breeding and caring for puppies entails. You must be prepared to assume the responsibility of caring for the mother through her pregnancy and for the puppies until they are of saleable age. Raising a litter of puppies can be a rewarding experience, but it means work as well as fun, and there is no guarantee of financial profit. As the puppies grow older and require more room and care, the amateur breeder, in desperation, often sells the puppies for much less than they are worth; sometimes he has to give them away. If the cost of keeping the puppies will drain your finances, think twice.

If you have given careful consideration to all these things and still want to breed your female, remember that there is some preparation necessary before taking this step.

## WHEN TO BREED

It is usually best to breed in the second or third season of your bitch. Consider when the puppies will be born and whether their birth and later care will interfere with your work or vacation plans. Gestation period is approximately fifty-eight to sixty-five days. Allow enough time to select

## NORMAL BITCH MATING CYCLE

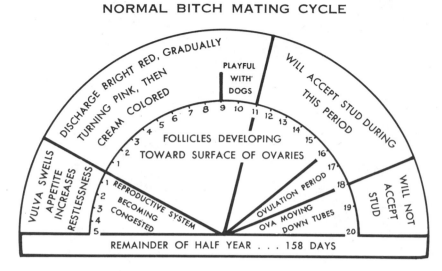

the right stud for her. Don't be in a position of having to settle for any available stud if she comes into season sooner than expected. Your female will probably be ready to breed twelve days after the first colored discharge. You can usually make arrangements to board her with the owner of the male for a few days to insure her being there at the proper time, or you can take her to be mated and bring her home the same day. If she still appears receptive she may be bred again a day or two later. Some females never show signs of willingness, so it helps to have the experience of a breeder. The second day after the discharge changes color is the proper time; she may be bred for about three days following. For an additional week or so she may have some discharge and attract other dogs by her odor, but she can seldom be bred at this time.

## HOW TO SELECT A STUD

Choose a mate for your female with an eye to countering her deficiencies. If possible, both male and female should have several ancestors in common within the last two or three generations, as such combinations generally "click" best. The male should have a good show record himself or be the sire of champions. The owner of the stud usually charges a fee for the use of the dog. The fee varies. Payment of a fee does not guarantee a litter, but it does generally confer the right to breed your female again to the stud if she does not have puppies the first time. In some cases the owner of the stud will agree to take a choice puppy in place of the stud fee. You and the owner of the stud should settle all details beforehand, including such questions as what age the puppies should reach before the

Maintenance of a state of excellent health is essential if you are contemplating breeding your bitch or stud. Poor health may not only interfere with reproductive processes but can actually rob your dog of his or her interest in mating. If you are not confident in commercial preparations, consult your vet for the best vitamin supplements to add to your dog's diet.

stud's owner can make his choice, what disposition is made of the single surviving puppy under an agreement by which the stud owner has the pick of the litter, and so on. In all cases, it is best that all agreements entered into by bitch owner and stud owner be in the form of a written contract.

It is customary for the female to be sent to the male. If the stud dog of your choice lives any distance from you, you will have to make arrangements to have your female shipped to him. The quickest way is by air, and if you call your nearest airport the airline people will give you information as to the best and fastest flight. Some airlines furnish their own crates for shipping, whereas others require that you furnish your own. The owner of the stud will make the arrangements for shipping the female back to you. You have to pay all shipping charges.

**PREPARATION FOR BREEDING**

Before you breed your female, make sure she is in good health. She should be neither too thin nor too fat. Skin diseases must be cured before breeding; a bitch with skin diseases can pass them on to her puppies. If

# Perpetual Whelping Chart

| | | | | | | | | | | | | | | | | | | | | | | | | | | | | | | | |
|---|---|---|---|---|---|---|---|---|---|---|---|---|---|---|---|---|---|---|---|---|---|---|---|---|---|---|---|---|---|---|---|
| Bred—Jan. | 1 | 2 | 3 | 4 | 5 | 6 | 7 | 8 | 9 | 10 | 11 | 12 | 13 | 14 | 15 | 16 | 17 | 18 | 19 | 20 | 21 | 22 | 23 | 24 | 25 | 26 | 27 | 28 | 29 | 30 | 31 |
| Due—March | 5 | 6 | 7 | 8 | 9 | 10 | 11 | 12 | 13 | 14 | 15 | 16 | 17 | 18 | 19 | 20 | 21 | 22 | 23 | 24 | 25 | 26 | 27 | 28 | 29 | 30 | 31 | Apr 1 | 2 | 3 | 4 |
| Bred—Feb. | 1 | 2 | 3 | 4 | 5 | 6 | 7 | 8 | 9 | 10 | 11 | 12 | 13 | 14 | 15 | 16 | 17 | 18 | 19 | 20 | 21 | 22 | 23 | 24 | 25 | 26 | 27 | 28 | | | |
| Due—April | 5 | 6 | 7 | 8 | 9 | 10 | 11 | 12 | 13 | 14 | 15 | 16 | 17 | 18 | 19 | 20 | 21 | 22 | 23 | 24 | 25 | 26 | 27 | 28 | 29 | 30 | May 1 | 2 | | | |
| Bred—Mar. | 1 | 2 | 3 | 4 | 5 | 6 | 7 | 8 | 9 | 10 | 11 | 12 | 13 | 14 | 15 | 16 | 17 | 18 | 19 | 20 | 21 | 22 | 23 | 24 | 25 | 26 | 27 | 28 | 29 | 30 | 31 |
| Due—May | 3 | 4 | 5 | 6 | 7 | 8 | 9 | 10 | 11 | 12 | 13 | 14 | 15 | 16 | 17 | 18 | 19 | 20 | 21 | 22 | 23 | 24 | 25 | 26 | 27 | 28 | 29 | 30 | 31 | June 1 | 2 |
| Bred—Apr. | 1 | 2 | 3 | 4 | 5 | 6 | 7 | 8 | 9 | 10 | 11 | 12 | 13 | 14 | 15 | 16 | 17 | 18 | 19 | 20 | 21 | 22 | 23 | 24 | 25 | 26 | 27 | 28 | 29 | 30 | |
| Due—June | 3 | 4 | 5 | 6 | 7 | 8 | 9 | 10 | 11 | 12 | 13 | 14 | 15 | 16 | 17 | 18 | 19 | 20 | 21 | 22 | 23 | 24 | 25 | 26 | 27 | 28 | 29 | 30 | July 1 | 2 | |
| Bred—May | 1 | 2 | 3 | 4 | 5 | 6 | 7 | 8 | 9 | 10 | 11 | 12 | 13 | 14 | 15 | 16 | 17 | 18 | 19 | 20 | 21 | 22 | 23 | 24 | 25 | 26 | 27 | 28 | 29 | 30 | 31 |
| Due—July | 3 | 4 | 5 | 6 | 7 | 8 | 9 | 10 | 11 | 12 | 13 | 14 | 15 | 16 | 17 | 18 | 19 | 20 | 21 | 22 | 23 | 24 | 25 | 26 | 27 | 28 | 29 | 30 | 31 | August 1 | 2 |
| Bred—June | 1 | 2 | 3 | 4 | 5 | 6 | 7 | 8 | 9 | 10 | 11 | 12 | 13 | 14 | 15 | 16 | 17 | 18 | 19 | 20 | 21 | 22 | 23 | 24 | 25 | 26 | 27 | 28 | 29 | 30 | |
| Due—August | 3 | 4 | 5 | 6 | 7 | 8 | 9 | 10 | 11 | 12 | 13 | 14 | 15 | 16 | 17 | 18 | 19 | 20 | 21 | 22 | 23 | 24 | 25 | 26 | 27 | 28 | 29 | 30 | 31 | Sept. 1 | |
| Bred—July | 1 | 2 | 3 | 4 | 5 | 6 | 7 | 8 | 9 | 10 | 11 | 12 | 13 | 14 | 15 | 16 | 17 | 18 | 19 | 20 | 21 | 22 | 23 | 24 | 25 | 26 | 27 | 28 | 29 | 30 | 31 |
| Due—September | 2 | 3 | 4 | 5 | 6 | 7 | 8 | 9 | 10 | 11 | 12 | 13 | 14 | 15 | 16 | 17 | 18 | 19 | 20 | 21 | 22 | 23 | 24 | 25 | 26 | 27 | 28 | 29 | 30 | Oct. 1 | 2 |
| Bred—Aug. | 1 | 2 | 3 | 4 | 5 | 6 | 7 | 8 | 9 | 10 | 11 | 12 | 13 | 14 | 15 | 16 | 17 | 18 | 19 | 20 | 21 | 22 | 23 | 24 | 25 | 26 | 27 | 28 | 29 | 30 | 31 |
| Due—October | 3 | 4 | 5 | 6 | 7 | 8 | 9 | 10 | 11 | 12 | 13 | 14 | 15 | 16 | 17 | 18 | 19 | 20 | 21 | 22 | 23 | 24 | 25 | 26 | 27 | 28 | 29 | 30 | 31 | Nov. 1 | 2 |
| Bred—Sept. | 1 | 2 | 3 | 4 | 5 | 6 | 7 | 8 | 9 | 10 | 11 | 12 | 13 | 14 | 15 | 16 | 17 | 18 | 19 | 20 | 21 | 22 | 23 | 24 | 25 | 26 | 27 | 28 | 29 | 30 | |
| Due—November | 3 | 4 | 5 | 6 | 7 | 8 | 9 | 10 | 11 | 12 | 13 | 14 | 15 | 16 | 17 | 18 | 19 | 20 | 21 | 22 | 23 | 24 | 25 | 26 | 27 | 28 | 29 | 30 | Dec. 1 | 2 | |
| Bred—Oct. | 1 | 2 | 3 | 4 | 5 | 6 | 7 | 8 | 9 | 10 | 11 | 12 | 13 | 14 | 15 | 16 | 17 | 18 | 19 | 20 | 21 | 22 | 23 | 24 | 25 | 26 | 27 | 28 | 29 | 30 | 31 |
| Due—December | 3 | 4 | 5 | 6 | 7 | 8 | 9 | 10 | 11 | 12 | 13 | 14 | 15 | 16 | 17 | 18 | 19 | 20 | 21 | 22 | 23 | 24 | 25 | 26 | 27 | 28 | 29 | 30 | 31 | Jan. 1 | 2 |
| Bred—Nov. | 1 | 2 | 3 | 4 | 5 | 6 | 7 | 8 | 9 | 10 | 11 | 12 | 13 | 14 | 15 | 16 | 17 | 18 | 19 | 20 | 21 | 22 | 23 | 24 | 25 | 26 | 27 | 28 | 29 | 30 | |
| Due—January | 3 | 4 | 5 | 6 | 7 | 8 | 9 | 10 | 11 | 12 | 13 | 14 | 15 | 16 | 17 | 18 | 19 | 20 | 21 | 22 | 23 | 24 | 25 | 26 | 27 | 28 | 29 | 30 | 31 | Feb. 1 | |
| Bred—Dec. | 1 | 2 | 3 | 4 | 5 | 6 | 7 | 8 | 9 | 10 | 11 | 12 | 13 | 14 | 15 | 16 | 17 | 18 | 19 | 20 | 21 | 22 | 23 | 24 | 25 | 26 | 27 | 28 | 29 | 30 | 31 |
| Due—February | 2 | 3 | 4 | 5 | 6 | 7 | 8 | 9 | 10 | 11 | 12 | 13 | 14 | 15 | 16 | 17 | 18 | 19 | 20 | 21 | 22 | 23 | 24 | 25 | 26 | 27 | 28 | March 1 | 2 | 3 | 4 |

she has worms she should be wormed before being bred, or within three weeks afterward. It is a good idea to have your veterinarian give her a booster shot for distemper and hepatitis before the puppies are born. This will increase the immunity the puppies receive during their early, most vulnerable period. Choose a dependable veterinarian and rely on him if there is an emergency when your female whelps.

Do not breed your bitch after she reaches six years of age. If you wish to breed her several times while she is young, it is wise to breed her only once a year. In other words, breed her, skip at least one season, and then breed her again. This will allow her to gain back her full strength between whelpings.

## THE IMPORTANCE AND APPLICATION OF GENETICS

Any person attempting to breed dogs should have a basic understanding of the transmission of traits, or characteristics, from the parents to the offspring and some familiarity with the more widely used genetic terms that he will probably encounter. A knowledge of the fundamental mechanics of genetics enables a breeder to better comprehend the passing on of good traits and bad from generation to generation and how a stud and bitch either complement or detract from each other's traits. It enables him to make a more judicial and scientific decision in selecting potential mates.

Inheritance, fundamentally, is due to the existence of microscopic units, known as *GENES,* present in the cells of all individuals. Genes somehow control the biochemical reactions that occur within the embryo or adult organism. This control results in changing or guiding the development of the organism's characteristics. A "string" of attached genes is known as a *CHROMOSOME.* With a few important exceptions, every chromosome has a partner chromosome carrying a duplicate or equivalent set of genes. Each gene, therefore, has a partner gene, known as an *ALLELE.* The number of different pairs of chromosomes present in the cells of the organism varies with the type of organism; a certain parasitic worm has only one pair, a certain fruit fly has four different pairs, man has 23 different pairs and your dog has 39 different pairs per cell. Because each chromosome may have many hundreds of genes, a single cell of the body may contain a total of several thousand genes. Heredity is obviously a very complex matter.

In the simplest form of genetic inheritance, one particular gene and its duplicate, or allele, on the partner chromosome control a single characteristic. The presence of freckles in the human skin, for example, is believed to be due to the influence of a single pair of genes.

Each cell of the body contains the specific number of paired

# FERTILIZATION

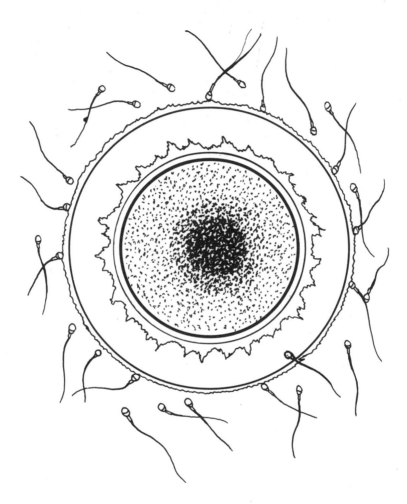

An egg, a special giant cell which the female ovaries produce, is being assaulted by sperm which are attempting to pierce the outer layer of the cell. Only one sperm cell penetration is necessary for fertilization. The first sperm to enter and reach the nucleus will bring with it the necessary chromosomes which will unite with those of the egg. With this union, the full complement of chromosomes necessary for the creation of a new fetus is complete. No other sperm cells are now able to penetrate the egg.

chromosomes characteristic of the organism. Because each type of gene is present on both chromosomes of a chromosome pair, each type of gene is therefore present in duplicate. The fusion of a sperm cell from the male with an egg cell from the female, as occurs in fertilization, should therefore result in offspring having a quadruplicate number (4) of each type of gene. Mating of these individuals would then produce progeny having an octuplicate number (8) of each type of gene, and so on. This, however, is normally prevented by a special process. When ordinary body cells prepare to divide to form more tissue, each pair of chromosomes duplicates itself so that there are four partner chromosomes of each kind instead of only two. When the cell divides, two of the four partners, or one pair, go into each new cell. This process, known as *MITOSIS,* insures that each new body cell contains the proper number of chromosomes. Reproductive cells (sperm and egg cells), however, undergo a special kind of division known as *MEIOSIS.* In meiosis, the chromosome pairs do not duplicate themselves, and thus when the reproductive cells reach the final dividing stage only one chromosome, or one-half of the pair, goes into each new reproductive cell. Each reproductive cell, therefore, has only half the normal number of chromosomes. These are referred to as *HAPLOID* cells, in contrast to *DIPLOID* cells, which have the full number of chromosomes. When the haploid sperm cell fuses with the haploid egg cell in fertilization, the resulting offspring has the normal diploid number of chromosomes.

If both partner genes, or alleles, affect the trait in an identical manner, the genes are said to be *HOMOZYGOUS,* but if one affects the character in a manner different from the other gene, or allele, the genes are said to be *HETEROZYGOUS.* For example, in the pair of genes affecting eye color in humans, if each gene of the pair produces blue eyes, while the other gene, or allele, produces brown eyes, they are said to be heterozygous. The presence of heterozygous genes raises the question, "Will the offspring have blue eyes or brown eyes?" which in turn introduces another genetic principle.

## DOMINANCE and RECESSIVENESS
If one gene of a pair can block the action of its partner, or allele, while still producing its own effect, that gene is said to be dominant over its allele. Its allele, on the other hand, is said to be recessive. In the case of heterozygous genes for eye color, the brown eye gene is dominant over the recessive blue eye gene, and the offspring therefore will have brown eyes. Much less common is the occurrence of gene pairs in which neither gene is completely dominant over the other. This, known as IN-COMPLETE or PARTIAL DOMINANCE, results in a blending of the

| SIRE and DAM | PROGENY |
|:---:|:---:|

## MENDELIAN EXPECTATION CHART

Pictured are the six possible ways in which a pair of genes can unite. The white boxes represent dominant genes; the black boxes represent recessives. Half of the genes of the sire will unite with half of the genes of the dam, and the expected results of such a mating are shown in the progeny combinations. Ratios apply to expectancy over large litters, except in lines 1, 2 and 6 where expectancy is realized in every litter (the exception due to mutation).

opposing influences. In cattle, if a homozygous (pure) red bull is mated with a homozygous (pure) white cow, the calf will be roan, a blending of red and white hairs in its coat, rather than either all red or all white.

During meiosis, or division of the reproductive (sperm and egg) cells, each pair of chromosomes splits, and one-half of each pair goes into one of the two new cells. Thus, in the case of eye color genes, one new reproductive cell will get the chromosome carrying the blue eye gene, while the other new reproductive cell will get the chromosome carrying the brown eye gene, and so on for each pair of chromosomes. If an organism has only one pair of chromosomes—called pair A, made up of chromosomes $A_1$ and $A_2$, and pair B, made up of chromosomes $B_1$ and $B_2$—each new reproductive cell will get one chromosome from each pair, and four different combinations are possible: $A_1$ and $B_1$; $A_1$ and $B_2$; $A_2$ and $B_1$; or $A_2$ and $B_2$. If the blue eye gene is on $A_1$, the brown eye gene on $A_2$, and the gene for curly hair on $B_1$, and the gene for straight hair on $B_2$, each of the above combinations will exert a different genetic effect on the offspring. This different grouping of chromosomes in the new reproductive cell as a result of meiotic cell division is known as *INDEPENDENT ASSORTMENT* and is one reason why variation occurs in the offspring. In the dog, with 39 pairs of chromosomes, the possibilites of variation through independent assortment are tremendous.

But variation does not end here. For example, if two dominant genes, such as the genes for brown eyes and dark hair, were on the same chromosome, all brown-eyed people would have dark hair. Yet in instances where such joined or *LINKED* genes do occur, the two characteristics do not always appear together in the same offspring. This is due to a process known as a *CROSS-OVER* or *RECOMBINATION*. Recombination is the mutual exchange of corresponding blocks of genes between the two chromosomes in a pair. That is, during cell division, the two chromosomes may exchange their tip sections or other corresponding segments. If the segments exchanged contain the eye color genes, the brown eye gene will be transferred from the chromosome carrying the dark hair gene to the chromosome carrying the light hair gene, and then brown eyes will occur with light hair, provided that the individual is homozygous for the recessive light hair gene.

Another important source of variation is *MUTATION*. In mutation, a gene becomes altered, such as by exposure to irradiation, and exerts a different effect than it did before. Most mutations are harmful to the organism, and some may result in death. Offspring carrying mutated genes and showing the effects of these mutations are known as *MUTANTS* or *SPORTS*. Mutation also means that instead of only two alleles for eye color, such as brown and blue, there may now be three or more (gray, black, etc.) creating a much larger source for possible variation in the offspring.

Further complications in the transmission and appearance of genetic traits are the phenomena known as *EPISTATIS* and *PLEIOTROPY*. Epistatis refers to a gene exerting influence on genes other than its own allele. In all-white red-eyed (albino) guinea pigs, for example, the gene controlling intensity of color is epistatic to any other color gene and prevents that gene from producing its effect. Thus, even if a gene for red spots were present in the cells of the guinea pig, the color intensity gene would prevent the red spots from appearing in the guinea pig's white coat. *Pleiotropy* refers to the fact that a single gene may control a number of characteristics. In the fruit fly, for example, the gene that controls eye color may also affect the structure of certain body parts and even the lifespan of the insect.

One special pair of chromosomes is known as the sex chromosomes. In man, dog, and other mammals, these chromosomes are of two types, designated as X and Y. Under normal conditions, a mammal carrying one X-type and one Y-type is a male. Females have two X chromosomes and can only contribute X chromosomes to the offspring, but the male can contribute either an X or a Y.

If the male's sperm carrying an X chromosome fertilizes the female's egg cell (X), the offspring (XX) will be a female; if a sperm carrying a Y chromosome fertilizes the egg (X), the offspring (XY) will be male. It is the male, therefore, that determines the sex of the offspring in mammals.

Traits controlled by genes present on the sex chromosome, and which appear in only one sex, are said to be SEX LINKED. If, for example, a rare recessive gene occurs on the X chromosome, it cannot exert its effect in the female because the dominant allele on the other X chromosomes will counteract it. In the male, however, there is no second X chromosome, and if the Y chromosome cannot offer any countereffect, the recessive character will appear. There are also SEX-LIMITED characteristics: these appear primarily or solely in one sex, but the genes for these traits are not carried on the sex chromosomes. Sex-limited traits appear when genes on other chromosomes exert their effect in the proper hormonal (male or female) environment. Sex-linked and sex-limited transmission is how a trait may skip a generation, by being passed from grandfather to grandson through a mother in which the trait, though present, does not show.

In dealing with the simplest form of heredity—one gene effecting one character—there is an expected ratio of the offspring displaying the character to those who do not display it, depending upon the genetic makeup of the parents. If a parent is homozygous for a character, such as blue eyes, it makes no difference which half of the chromosome pair enters the new reproductive cell, because each chromosome carries the gene for blue eyes. If a parent is heterozygous, however, one reproductive cell will receive the brown eye gene while the other will receive the blue eye gene. If both parents are homozygous for blue eyes, all the offspring will receive two blue eye genes, and all will have blue eyes. If a parent is homozygous for blue eyes, and the other parent is homozygous for brown eyes, all the offspring will be heterozygous, receiving one brown eye and one blue eye gene, and because brown is dominant, all will have brown eyes. If both parents are heterozygous, both the blue eye gene and the brown eye gene from one parent have an equal likelihood of ending up with either the blue eye or the brown eye gene from the other parent. This results in a ratio of two heterozygous offspring to the one homozygous for brown eyes and one homozygous for blue eyes, giving a total genetic, or genotypic, ratio of 2:1:1 or, as it is more commonly arranged, 1:2:1. As the two heterozygous as well as the homozygous brown eye offspring will have brown eyes, the ratio of brown eyes to blue eyes (or phenotypic ratio) will be 3:1.

If one parent is heterozygous and the other parent is homozygous for the recessive gene for blue eyes, but the other half of the offspring will be heterozygous and have brown eyes. (Here both the genotypic and phenotypic ratio is 1:1.)

If the homozygous parent, however, has the dominant gene (brown eyes), half of the offspring will be heterozygous and half will be homozygous, as before, but all will have brown eyes. By repeated determinations of these ratios in the offspring, geneticists are able to analyze the genetic makeup of the parents.

Before leaving heredity, it might be well to explain the difference between inbreeding, outcrossing, line breeding, and similar terms. Basically, there are only inbreeding and outbreeding. Inbreeding, however, according to its intensity, is usually divided into interbreeding proper and line breeding. Inbreeding proper is considered to be the mating of very closely related individuals, generally within the immediate family, but this is sometimes extended to include matings to first cousins and grandparents. Line breeding is the mating of more distantly related animals, that is, animals not immediately related to each other but having a common ancestor, such as the same grandsire or great-grandsire. Outbreeding is divided into outcrossing, which is the mating of dogs from different families within the same breed, and cross-breeding, which is mating purebred dogs from different breeds.

From the foregoing discussion of genetics, it should be realized that the theory of telegony, which states that the sire of one litter can influence future litters sired by other studs, is simply not true; it is possible, however, if several males mate with a female during a single estrus cycle, that the various puppies in the litter may have different sires (but not two sires for any one puppy). It should also be realized that blood does not really enter into the transmission of inheritance, although people commonly speak of "bloodlines," "pure-blooded," etc.

# 7. CARE OF THE MOTHER AND THE NEW FAMILY

## PRENATAL CARE OF THE FEMALE

You can expect the puppies nine weeks from the day of breeding, although 58 days is as common as 63. During this time the female should receive normal care and exercise. If she is overweight, don't increase her food at first; excess weight at whelping time is not good. If she is on the thin side, build her up, giving her a morning meal of cereal and egg yolk. Consult your veterinarian as to increasing her vitamins and mineral supplement. During the last weeks the puppies grow enormously, and the mother will have little room for food and less appetite. Divide her meals into smaller portions and feed her more often. If she loses her appetite, tempt her with meat, liver, chicken, etc.

As she grows heavier, eliminate violent exercise and jumping. Do not eliminate exercise entirely, as walking is beneficial to the female in whelp, and mild exercise will maintain her muscle tone in preparation for the birth. Weigh your female after breeding and keep a record of her weight each week thereafter. Groom your bitch daily—some females have a slight discharge during gestation, more prevalent during the last two weeks, so wash the vulva with warm water daily. Usually, by the end of the fifth week you can notice a broadening across her loins, and her breasts become firmer. By the end of the sixth week your veterinarian can tell you whether or not she is pregnant.

## PREPARATION OF WHELPING QUARTERS

Prepare a whelping box a few days before the puppies are due, and allow the mother to sleep there overnight or to spend some time in it during the day to become accustomed to it. Then she is less likely to try to have her pups under the front porch or in the middle of your bed. The box should have a wooden floor. Sides about a foot high will keep the puppies in but enable the mother to get out after she has fed them. If the weather is cold, the box should be raised about an inch off the floor.

You should place a guard rail in the whelping box to prevent the mother from rolling over onto the pups and smothering them. This guard is a strip of wood which will project out and above the floor of the box, keeping the bitch from pressing up against the sides of the box.

GUARD RAIL

SIDE BOARDS · ADDED LATER

STEP

ONE SIDE HINGED
FOR EASY CLEANING

**WHELPING BOX**

Layers of newspaper spread over the whole area will make excellent bedding and be absorbent enough to keep the surface warm and dry. They should be removed daily and replaced with another thick layer. An old quilt or washable blanket makes better footing for the nursing puppies than slippery newspaper during the first week, and is softer for the mother. The quilt should be secured firmly.

## SUPPLIES TO HAVE ON HAND

As soon as you have the whelping box prepared, set up the nursery by collecting the various supplies you will need when the puppies arrive. You should have the following items on hand: a box lined with towels for the puppies, a heating pad or hot water bottle to keep the puppy box warm, a pile of clean terrycloth towels or washcloths to remove membranes and to dry puppies, a stack of folded newspapers, a roll of paper towels, vaseline, rubber gloves, soap, iodine, muzzle, cotton balls, a small pair of blunt scissors to cut umbilical cords (place scissors into an open bottle of alcohol so they keep freshly sterilized), a rectal thermometer, white thread, a flashlight in case the electricity goes off, a waste container, and a scale for weighing each puppy at birth.

It is necessary that the whelping room be warm and free from drafts, because puppies are delivered wet from the mother. Keep a little notebook and pencil handy so you can record the duration of the first labor and the time between the arrival of each puppy. If there is trouble in whelping, this is the information that the veterinarian will want. Keep his telephone number handy in case you have to call him in an emergency, and warn him to be prepared for an emergency, should you need him.

## WHELPING

Be prepared for the actual whelping several days in advance. Usually the female will tear up papers, try to dig nests, refuse food, and generally act restless and nervous. These may be false alarms; the real test is her temperature, which will drop to below 100°F about twelve hours before whelping. Take her temperature rectally at a set time each day, starting about a week before she is due to whelp. After her temperature goes down, keep her constantly with you or put her in the whelping box and stay in the room with her. She will seem anxious and look to you for reassurance. During the birth, if neccesary, be prepared to remove the membranes covering the puppy's head if the mother fails to do this, for the puppy could smother otherwise.

The mother should start licking the puppy as soon as it is out of the sac, thus drying and stimulating it, but if she does not perform this task you can do it with a rough towel, instead. The afterbirth should follow the birth of each puppy, attached to the puppy by the umbilical cord. Watch to make sure that each is expelled, for retaining this material can cause infection. The mother probably will eat the afterbirth after biting the cord. One or two will not hurt her; they stimulate milk supply as well as labor for remaining puppies. Too many, however, can make her lose her appetite for the food she needs to feed her puppies and regain her strength, so remove the rest of them along with the soiled newspaper, and keep the box dry and clean to relieve her anxiety.

If a puppy does not start breathing, wrap him in a towel, hold him upside down with his head toward the ground, and shake him vigorously. If he still does not breathe, rub his ribs briskly; if this also fails, administer artificial respiration by compressing his ribs about twenty times per minute.

If the mother does not bite the cord, or bites it too close to the body, you should take over the job to prevent an umbilical hernia. Cut the cord a short distance from the body with your blunt scissors. Put a drop of iodine on the end of the cord; it will dry up and fall off in a few days.

The puppies should follow each other at regular intervals, but deliveries can be as short as five minutes or as long as two hours apart. A puppy may be presented backwards; if the mother does not seem to be in trouble, *do not interfere.* But if enough of the puppy is outside the birth canal, use a rough towel and help her by pulling gently on the puppy.

Pull only when she pushes. A rear-first, or breech birth can cause a puppy to strangle on its own umbilical cord, so don't let the mother struggle too long. Breech birth is quite common.

When you think all the puppies have been whelped, have your veterinarian examine the mother to determine if all the afterbirths have been expelled. He will probably give her an injection to be certain that the uterus is clean, a shot of calcium for prevention of eclampsia, and possibly an injection of penicillin to prevent infection.

## CAESAREAN SECTION

Sometimes a Caesarean section is necessary, although very rarely. The operation of removing the pups by cutting into the abdomen and uterus of the bitch is generally safe; however, if the emergency Caesarean section follows a prolonged, exhausting and fruitless labor, the danger to the bitch is substantially increased.

Reasons for resorting to a Caesarean section include: 1. dystocia due to an abnormally large pup, 2. one presenting in such a way that it cannot get out, is blocking the passage and birth of its littermates or is threatening the life of its dam, 3. an abnormal pelvis in the bitch which does not allow passage of the pups (such as a previous pelvic fracture), 4. inertia, 5. long and arduous labor which exhausts the bitch to the point where weakness causes the uterine and abdominal contractions to stop.

Your bitch can be operated on without losing consciousness if your veterinarian selects to operate with a hypnotic and local anesthesia. The local anesthesia is injected, the incision made, and the pups taken from the semi-conscious bitch.

Gas anesthesia is the safest type of general anesthetic for delivering pups; if barbiturate anesthetics are used intravenously, the puppies may be quite effected by these drugs as they pass through the placental barrier.

Regardless of which method is used for the Caesarean section, the patient should be kept in a warm, clean bed after surgery until she recovers from the anesthesia. The pups should not be placed with the dam until she is once again alert. If the pups are also depressed from the anesthetic, artificial respiration may be required. It is imperative that the pups be kept dry and warm following the delivery.

Offer the puppies to their mother one at a time. After she licks a pup, help it to get settled on a teat and observe them carefully. Rarely, the bitch may not accept her puppies, but this may only be a temporary situation. Watch the mother when she goes out to do her duties; her sutures (stitches) should not be subjected to any undue strain. A binder may interfere with emptying several breasts, but aside from this she will behave in a normal manner. The stitches will be removed in about two weeks and she will be as good as new.

In the cases of both normal and Caesarean delivery the female's temperature should be checked twice daily for one week after delivery. A temperature of over 102°F should be reported to your veterinarian and his directions followed to the letter.

## ECLAMPSIA

Eclampsia, or "milk fever," is caused by a lowered calcium content of the blood, due to the bitch's depleting her body's calcium reserves for the production of milk. It is a word that has been fearsome in the dog-breeding world for many years. If it occurs after whelping, the puppies and the mother are in severe danger. Help must be given immediately. The female stiffens her legs, has pale gums, and is likely to have minor convulsions. Puppies must be taken from her and calcium and dextrose administered to her intravenously. However, this is a rare thing and the symptoms so obvious, that assuredly the owner's first thought is that something is wrong and that the veterinarian is needed at once. With proper nutrition during gestation and lactation, a lack of calcium is not to be expected. The best preventive medicine is to see that the female is parasite free, in good condition, and properly cared for from the day she is mated.

## HOW TO TAKE CARE OF A LARGE LITTER

The size of a litter varies greatly. If your bitch has a large litter she may have trouble feeding all of the puppies. You can help her by preparing an extra puppy box. Leave half the litter with the mother and the other half in a warm place, changing their places at two-hour intervals at first. Later you may change them less frequently, leaving them all together except during the day. Try supplementary feeding, too, as soon as their eyes are open, since at about two weeks they will lap from a dish.

## RAISING THE PUPPIES

Hold each puppy to a breast as soon as he is dry, for a good meal without competition. Then he may join his littermates in the basket, out of his mother's way, while she is whelping. Keep a supply of evaporated milk on hand for emergencies, or later weaning. A formula of evaporated milk, corn syrup and a little water with egg yolk should be warmed and fed in a doll or baby bottle if necessary. A supplementary feeding often helps weak pups over the hump. Keep track of birth weights and take weekly readings so you will have an accurate record of the pups' growth and health.

This compartmentalized incubator demonstrates one method of caring for orphaned puppies. Orphaned pups need to be kept warm by artificial means since they do not have their mother to cuddle next to.

After the puppies have arrived, take the mother outside for a walk and drink, and then leave her to take care of them. She will probably not want to stay away more than a minute or two for the first few weeks. Be sure to keep water available at all times, and feed her milk or broth frequently, as she needs liquids to produce milk. To encourage her to eat, offer her the foods she likes best, until she asks to be fed without your tempting her. She will soon develop a ravenous appetite and should have at least two large meals a day, with dry food available in addition.

Prepare a warm place to put the puppies after they are born to keep them dry and help them to a good start in life. Cover an electric heating pad or hot-water bottle with flannel and put it in the bottom of a cardboard box. Set the box near the mother so that she can see her puppies. She will usually allow you to help, but don't take the puppies out of sight, and let her handle things if your interference seems to make her nervous.

Be sure that all of the puppies are getting enough to eat. If the mother sits or stands, instead of lying still to nurse, the probable cause is scratching from the puppies's nails. You can remedy this by clipping them, as you do hers. Manicure scissors will do for these tiny claws.

The puppies should normally be completely weaned at six weeks, although you start to feed them at three weeks. They will find it easier to lap semi-solid food. At four weeks they will eat four meals a day, and soon do without their mother entirely. Start them on mixed dog food, or leave it with them in a dish for self-feeding. Don't leave water with them all the time; at this age everything is to play with and they will use it as a wading pool. They can drink all they need if it is offered several times a day, after meals.

As the puppies grow up the mother will go into the pen only to nurse them, first sitting up and then standing. To dry her up completely, keep the mother away for longer periods, and then completely. The little milk left will be reabsorbed.

## AIRING THE PUPPIES

The puppies may be put outside, unless it is too cold, as soon as their eyes are open. They will benefit from the sunlight and the vitamin D it provides. A rubber mat or newspapers underneath will protect them from cold or damp.

## WORMING

You can expect a litter of pups to need at least one worming before they are ready to go to new homes, so take a stool sample to your veterinarian at about six weeks of age. Also, the litter should receive their first temporary shots, which are usually distemper-hepatitis-leptospirosis globulin. Today many kennels are advised by veterinarians to administer these preventative shots even earlier than six weeks, and in special cases they may begin right after birth. The puppy derives immunity from his mother's milk during the first twenty-four hours of his life; this immunity lasts for a varying length of time. Some mothers do not offer any immunity to their young at all. Therefore, in a kennel where the exposure rate is high, and many dogs come and go to shows, and disease may easily be brought to the premises, prophylactic treatment must start early. In the average home, where there is one female and one litter, six weeks is the proper time to start this treatment, and it must be repeated every one to two weeks until the puppies are old enough to have their permanent shots.

## PUPPY SOCIALIZATION

Animal psychologists, research scientists and people who train dogs to work closely with people, such as trainers of seeing-eye dogs, have found that the first few weeks of a puppy's life is a critical time. The treatment a puppy receives during this stage determines whether he will become a mentally stable, trustworthy dog that likes people and is able to fit into their particular lifestyle. In general, the dog that is to be a reliable show dog or loving pet must be cuddled often, and experience pleasurable associations with people from a very early age. It is the duty of every creditable breeder to be willing to commit the amount of time necessary to socialize his puppies before he decides to breed his bitch. The behavior of his puppies, whether they are show prospects or pets, reflects on the breed and on his kennel name, two very good reasons for giving the puppies the kind of exposure to human companionship that will turn them into desirable adult dogs. This is not to deny heredity, but to stress the importance of human association in the early weeks of a puppy's life.

Some experts feel that the first three weeks of a puppy's life are completely taken up with nursing, sleeping and keeping warm snuggling with his littermates and dam, and that people-geared socialization should begin after these first three weeks. Others feel that it should begin right away, but that the form varies with the age. During the first weeks while the puppy is still gaining strength and weight and until his eyes are open, socialization should consist of simply holding the tiny pup, stroking its back and tummy for a few minutes and then putting it back with its mother. This should take place with each puppy, every day. As the puppy grows older, the time can be lengthened.

When the puppies are old enough to start eating solid foods, you can reinforce the pleasure contact by feeding them by hand. Basic training and developing receptivity to further training when they are older takes place at this point, so when you call them to you for the hand-held food, **always use the same catch phrase. When the puppies are about a month** old it's time to reinforce their sense of self-sufficiency and ease in new surroundings. This will also ease the transition to a new home. Remove the pups from their whelping box, which until now has circumscribed nearly their entire world, and take them to a different scene. The pup with the most adaptable nature is the one who will immediately move about and begin to explore this new setting. Puppies that are frightened and do not relax after a short time in this new environment should be put back with their mates until next time.

When they are six weeks old, puppies can be further disposed to training by putting a collar on them so they will get used to the feeling of it. Then put on the leash, not to take them for a walk, but just to let them run around in it so they get used to the idea. Later, more serious training can take place by the new owner with the puppy that is taking his place as a temperamentally sound, self-assured, friendly youngster in the world of his human companions.

# 8. GENERAL HEALTH CARE

## WATCHING YOUR PUPPY'S HEALTH

First, don't be frightened by the number of diseases a dog can contract. The majority of dogs never get any of them. Don't become a dog-hypochondriac. All dogs have days when they feel lazy and want to lie around doing nothing. For the few diseases that you might be concerned about, remember that your veterinarian is your dog's best friend. When you first get your puppy, select a veterinarian whom you have faith in. He will get to know your dog and will be glad to have you consult him for advice. A dog needs little medical care, but that little is essential to his good health and well-being. He needs:

1. Proper diet at regular hours
2. Clean, roomy housing
3. Daily exercise
4. Companionship and love
5. Frequent grooming
6. Regular check-ups by your veterinarian

## THE USEFUL THERMOMETER

Almost every serious ailment shows itself by an increase in the dog's body temperature. If your dog acts lifeless, looks dull-eyed, and gives the impression of illness, check his temperature by using a rectal thermometer. A stubby end rectal thermometer of either plastic or glass is best suited for this procedure. Although uncommon, there is always the hazard of possible breakage should he become excited during insertion. However, he is easily calmed if you soothe him when the routine is taking place. Hold the dog securely, and insert the thermometer, which you have lubricated with vaseline, and take a reading. The average normal temperature for your dog will be 101.5°F. Excitement may raise the temperature slightly, but any rise of more than a few points is cause for alarm, and your vet should be consulted.

## EMERGENCY FIRST AID

In general, a dog will heal his wounds by licking them. If he swallows anything harmful, chances are that he will throw it up. But it will probably make you feel better to help him if he is hurt, so treat his wounds as you would your own. Wash out the dirt and apply an antiseptic.

If you fear that your dog has swallowed poison, get him to the veterinarian's *at once*. In the meantime, try and locate the source of poisoning; if he has swallowed, for example, a cleaning fluid kept in your house, check the bottle label to see if inducing the dog to vomit is necessary. In some cases, inducing the dog to vomit can be very harmful, depending upon the type of poison swallowed. Amateur diagnosis is very dangerous, when you consider that time is so extremely important.

## Accidents

Accidents, unfortunately, will happen so it is best to be prepared. If your dog gets hit by a car, keep him absolutely quiet, move him as little as possible and get veterinary treatment as soon as possible. It is unwise to give any stimulants such as brandy or other alcoholic liquids where there is visible external hemorrhage or the possibility of internal hemorrhaging. If your dog has cut his foot or leg badly, on glass or otherwise, bandage the wound as tightly as possible to stop the bleeding. A wad of cotton may serve as a pressure bandage, which will ordinarily stop the flow of blood. Gauze wrapped around the cotton will hold it in place. Usually, applying such pressure to a wound will sufficiently stop the blood flow; however, for severe bleeding, such as when an artery is cut, a tourniquet may be necessary. Apply a tourniquet between the injury and the heart if the bleeding is severe. To tighten the tourniquet, push a pencil through the bandage and twist it. Take your dog to a veterinarian immediately since a tourniquet should not be left in place any longer than fifteen minutes.

Blood coming from an artery is bright red in color and will spurt in unison with the heart beat. From a vein, it is dark red and continuous in flow.

## Burns and Scalds

Any dog kept in the home runs the risk of being burned or scalded at one time or another. If your pet sustains a serious burn, call the vet immediately as shock quickly follows such a burn. The dog should be kept warm and quiet, wrapped in a blanket. If he still shows signs of being chilled, use a hot water bottle. Clean the burn gently, removing any foreign matter such as bits of lint, hair, grass or dirt. Act as quickly as possible. Prevent exposure to air by applying olive oil or another similar substance and cover with gauze, cotton and a loose bandage. To prevent the dog from interfering with the dressing, muzzle him and have someone stay with him until veterinary treatment is at hand.

If the burn or scald is a minor one clip hair away from the affected area and apply a paste of bicarbonate of soda and water. Apply it thickly to the burned area and try to keep the dog from licking it off.

Often the only way to adequately determine the best treatment for your dog is through microscopic analysis of a blood smear or tissue scraping so the veterinarian can diagnose the ailment exactly.

### Snake Bite

If your dog is bitten by a poisonous snake, open up the wound with any available instrument that is sharp and clean. Squeeze the wound to cause a fair amount of blood to flow. This will wash the poison from the wound as much as possible. The dog should be taken to the veterinarian immediately so antitoxins can be administered. If the bite has been sustained on the leg, it is advisable to apply a tourniquet if at all possible to keep the poison from flowing further. Under no circumstances should snake bite from a poisonous snake, or its treatment, be taken lightly.

### Stings

Many dogs enjoy trying to catch wasps and bees. When these insects are prevalent it is difficult to stop your pet from snapping at them. A sting frequently follows a successful catch and it often occurs inside the mouth, which can be very serious. The best remedy is to get him to a veterinarian as soon as possible, but there are some precautionary measures to follow in the meantime. If the dog has been lucky enough to only be caught on the outside of the face, try to extricate the stinger, then swab the point of entry with a solution of bicarbonate of soda. In the case of a wasp sting, use vinegar or some other acidic food stuff. A useful remedy for wasp stings is to rub the part with moistened tobacco, i.e., an unsmoked cigarette end that has been moistened.

## IMPORTANCE OF INOCULATIONS

With the proper series of inoculations, your dog will be almost completely protected against disease. However, it occasionally happens that the shot does not take, and sometimes a different form of the virus appears against which your dog may not be protected.

### Distemper

Probably the most virulent of all dog diseases is distemper. Young dogs are most susceptible to it, although it may affect dogs of all ages. The dog will lose his appetite, seem depressed, chilled, and run a fever. Often he will have a watery discharge from his eyes and nose. Unless treated promptly, the disease goes into advanced stages with infections of the lungs, intestines, and nervous system, and dogs that recover may be left with some impairment such as paralysis, convulsions, a twitch, or some other defect, usually spastic in nature. The best protection against this is very early inoculation with a series of permanent shots and a booster shot each year thereafter.

### Hepatitis

Veterinarians report an increase in the spread of this viral disease in recent years, usually with younger dogs as the victims. The initial symptoms—drowsiness, vomiting, great thirst, loss of appetite, and a high temperature—closely resemble those of distemper. These symptoms are often accompanied by swellings of the head, neck, and abdomen. The disease strikes quickly; death may occur in just a few hours. Protection is afforded by injection with a vaccine recently developed.

### Leptospirosis

This disease is carried by bacteria that live in stagnant or slow-moving water. It is carried by rats and dogs; infection is begun by the dog's licking substances contaminated by the urine or feces of infected animals. The symptoms are diarrhea and a yellowish-brownish discoloration of the jaws, tongue, and teeth, caused by an inflammation of the kidneys.

This disease can be cured if caught in time, but it is best to ward it off with a vaccine which your veterinarian can administer along with the distemper shots.

## Rabies

This is an acute disease of the dog's central nervous system. It is spread by infectious saliva transmitted by the bite of an infected animal. Rabies is generally manifested in one of two classes of symptoms. The first is "furious rabies," in which the dog shows a period of melancholy or depression, then irritation, and finally paralysis. The first period lasts from a few hours to several days. During this time the dog is cross and will change his position often. He loses his appetite for food and begins to lick, bite and swallow foreign objects. During the irritative phase the dog is spasmodically wild and has impulses to run away. He acts in a fearless manner and runs at and bites everything in sight. If he is caged or confined he will fight at the bars, often breaking teeth or fracturing his jaw. His bark becomes a peculiar howl. In the final, or paralytic, stage, the animal's lower jaw becomes paralyzed and hangs down; he walks with a stagger and saliva drips from his mouth. Within four to eight days after the onset of paralysis, the dog dies.

The second class of symptoms is referred to as "dumb rabies" and is characterized by the dog's walking in a bearlike manner, head down. The lower jaw is paralyzed and the dog is unable to bite. Outwardly, it may seem as though he had a bone caught in his throat.

Even if your pet should be bitten by a rabid dog or other animal, he probably can be saved if you get him to the veterinarian in time for a series of injections. However, after the symptoms have appeared no cure is possible. But remember that an annual rabies inoculation is almost certain protection against rabies. If you suspect that your dog has rabies, notify your local Health Department. A rabid dog is a danger to all who come near him.

## Canine Parvovirus

This highly contagious virus disease has recently joined the ranks of potential canine killers and has spread in almost epidemic proportions throughout certain sections of the United States. It has appeared in Canada, Australia and Europe as well. CPV attacks the intestinal tract, white blood cells, and less frequently the heart muscle. It is believed to spread through dog-to-dog contact, the specific source of infection being the fecal waste matter of infected dogs. CPV is particularly hard to overcome because it is capable of existing in the environment for many months under varying conditions unless strong disinfectants are used.

CPV's high degree of contagion is augmented by the fact that it can readily be transmitted from place to place on the hair and feet of infected dogs. Contact with contaminated cages, shoes, and the like can also transmit CPV. However, while it is highly contagious among dogs, the disease cannot be contracted by other animals or people from infected dogs.

The initial signs of infection of this viral disease are normally vomiting and severe diarrhea, which will appear within five to seven days after the individual has been exposed to the virus. At the onset of illness, feces will be light gray or yellow-gray in color. Occasionally, the dog's diarrheal waste will be blood-streaked. Because of the vomiting and severe diarrhea, the dog that has contracted the disease will dehydrate quickly. Depression and loss of appetite can accompany the other symptoms as well as a rise in temperature in younger dogs especially. Temperatures may range from 104 degrees to 106. Older dogs may suffer no temperature increase at all and generally CPV is fatal in only two to three percent of those afflicted.

Death caused by this disease normally occurs within 48 to 72 hours following the appearance of the symptoms. Puppies are hardest hit, with the virus being fatal to 75 percent of puppies that contract it. Death is almost shock-like in their case and can occur within two days of the onset of the illness.

The best preventive measure for CPV is vaccination administered by your veterinarian. Consult him about the duration of immunity of each inoculation and for a schedule of future inoculations. Precautionary measures individual pet owners can take include disinfecting the kennel and other areas where the dog is housed. Since the virus is hardy and capable of existing for many months, a strong disinfectant must be used. One part sodium hypochlorite solution (household bleach), to 30 parts of water will do the job efficiently. Keep the dog from coming into contact with the fecal matter of other dogs when walking or exercising your pet.

## HIP DYSPLASIA

This often crippling condition is more prevalent in large breeds than in small, but has occurred in almost every breed. The cause is not absolutely known though it is believed to be hereditary and as yet there is no known cure. The condition exists in varying degrees of severity. In general, hip dysplasia can be described as a poor fit between the two bones of the hip joint—the femur and the acetabulum—and is caused by a malformation of one or the other. Either the head of the femur is flattened causing it to slip out of the socket, or a shallowness of the acetabulum causes the femur to slip out. HD is usually graded according to severity and poorness of fit between the ball and socket, with the lowest grades being the best fit and the higher end of the scale denoting the worst cases.

HD causes stiffness in the hindlegs, considerable pain in the more severe cases and difficulty of movement. It generally manifests itself in puppyhood and can be noticed by the time the young dog is two months old. Severity can usually be determined by the age of six months. If HD is suspected, the dog should be x-rayed, and if afflicted it should not be used for breeding. Cases vary greatly, but severe pain may be more or less continuous in advanced cases. When this is true euthanasia is occasionally recommended, though medication is available to control the pain and allow the dog to move with more ease. Rigorous exercise is not recommended since it only increases the rate at which the bone surfaces wear away.

## COUGHS, COLDS, BRONCHITIS, PNEUMONIA

Respiratory diseases may affect the dog because he is forced to live under man-made conditions rather than in his natural environment. Being subjected to cold or a draft after a bath, sleeping near an air conditioner or in the path of a fan or near a radiator can cause respiratory ailments. The symptoms are similar to those in humans. The germs of these diseases, however, are different and do not affect both dogs and humans, so they cannot be infected by each other. Treatment is much the same as for a child with the same type of illness. Keep the dog warm, quiet, and well fed. Your veterinarian has antibiotics and other remedies to help the dog recover.

## DIABETES MELLITUS (Sugar Diabetes)

This is a disease wherein the sugar balance of the body is disturbed because of insufficient production of the hormone insulin. The pancreas secretes insulin which regulates carbohydrate/sugar usage. When the insulin-producing cells are damaged, the condition arises. It is marked by an increase in the blood sugar level and an excessive amount of sugar is excreted in the urine.

Symptoms of the condition are great thirst, increased urination and loss of weight while the appetite and food consumption increases. The signs vary in severity. If overlooked, emaciation and collapse rapidly occur. The dog can go into a diabetic coma and die.

Treatment is the same as for human diabetes, utilizing dietary regulation and insulin injections if necessary. The diet should be one of very low fat, with a low percentage of carbohydrate and a higher pecentage of protein. The insulin dose must be adjusted as indicated by urine tests which your veterinarian can teach you to administer at home. The test makes use of chemically treated sticks, pale yellow in color, which turn to various shades of green when dipped in urine. The darker the shade, the more serious the condition.

## INTERNAL PARASITES

There are four common internal parasites that may infect your dog. These are roundworms, hookworms, whipworms, and tapeworms. The first three can be diagnosed by laboratory examination; the presence of tapeworms is determined by seeing segments in the stool or attached to the hair around the tail. Do not under any circumstances attempt to worm your dog without the advice of your veterinarian. After first determining what type of worm or worms are present, he will advise you of the best method of treatment.

A dog or puppy in good physical condition is less susceptible to worm infestation than a weak dog. Proper sanitation and a nutritious diet help in preventing worms. One of the best preventative measures is to always have clean, dry bedding for your dog. This will diminish the possibility of reinfection due to flea or tick bites.

### Heartworms

Heartworm infestation in dogs is passed by mosquitoes and can be a life threatening problem. Dogs with the disease tire easily, have difficulty breathing, cough and may lose weight despite a hearty appetite. If caught in the early stages, the disease can be effectively treated; however, the administration of daily preventative medicine throughout the spring, summer and fall months is strongly advised. Your veterinarian must first take

Pictured is the heart of a dog showing a heavy infestation of heartworms. Mosquitoes carry the offspring of the adult worms which are implanted into a dog's bloodstream when the dog is bitten. The worm offspring travel to the heart where they do their damage as they develop into adult worms. U.S.D.A.

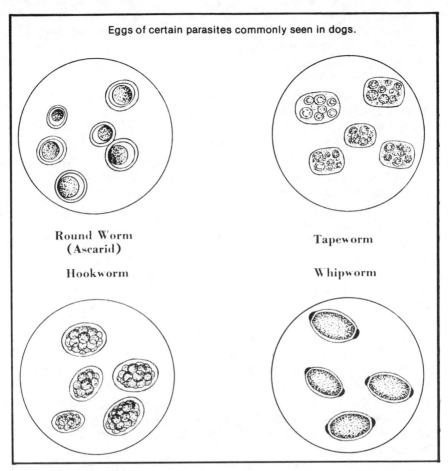

Eggs of certain parasites commonly seen in dogs.

Round Worm
(Ascarid)

Tapeworm

Hookworm

Whipworm

The presence of worms in your dog's system can manifest itself in outward signs such as a general deterioration, loss of weight, dulling of coat, diarrhea and vomiting. *Roundworm* larvae penetrate the intestinal lining, where they enter the bloodstream and are carried to the lungs. This worm affects mostly puppies, in whom it can cause lung damage and intestinal blockage. There are many species of *tapeworm* that can infest your dog. The important factor in breaking the life cycle of the tapeworm is the elimination of the parasitic host on which the worm thrives. Fleas are perhaps the most common host, so ridding your dog of them is a step toward eliminating the possibility of tapeworm infection. If present in massive quantities, *hookworms*, which remove blood from the dog, may cause circulatory collapse and ultimate death. *Whipworms* may cause weight loss, vomiting, diarrhea and secondary anemia in an affected dog.

a blood sample from your dog to test for the presence of the disease, and if the dog is heartworm-free, pills or liquid medicine can be prescribed that will protect against any infestation.

It was formerly believed that heartworms occured only in warmer climates, but it is now known that they may occur anywhere that they can be carried by any of several species of mosquitoes.

Adult worms are found in the right side of the heart, the vena cavae and the pulmonary artery. There the eggs develop and are released as microfilariae. The microfilariae circulate in the blood of the dog until a mosquito ingests them, starting the larval growth cycle. Being carried by the various mosquito species induces the third-stage larval development. The third-stage larvae are re-deposited during a subsequent feeding by the mosquito and proceed to grow.

Microfilariae remain inactive while in the blood of the dog in which they were originally deposited by the female. It is only after they have been ingested by a subsequent mosquito and redeposited in another host that they begin to develop. These larvae lodge in subcutaneous tissue or muscle where they stay about three months; at between three and four months they migrate to the heart. Three to four months later the adult worm begins producing microfilariae.

Adult worms are creamy white in color. The female grows to 11 or 12 inches in length, the male, to six or seven inches. The sexes are distinquished by length since both are about the diameter of the lead in a mechanical pencil. Each mature female worm is capable of producing 30,000 microfilariae each day. A hundred adult females can account for about two billion microfilariae in the body of a dog since microfilariae live up to two years.

Apparently canines of all ages are susceptible to heartworm infestation, but they must have been exposed to mosquitoes in order to have acquired the third-stage infective larvae. Heartworm infection increases markedly as the dog matures. If left undetected, it will erode the heart.

A microscopic search for microfilariae is necessary to prove that adult worms are present. Because of the large number and size of the worms, treatment must be careful and slow to minimize damage to the circulatory system.

## SKIN AILMENTS

Any persistent scratching may indicate an irritation. Whenever you groom your dog, look for the reddish spots that may indicate eczema, mange, or fungal infection. Rather than treating your dog yourself, take him to the veterinarian, as some of the conditions may be difficult to eradicate and can cause permanent damage to his coat.

Two of the most common external parasites are the tick (left) and the flea (right). Along with the general discomfort and irritation that they bring to your dog, these parasites can infest him with worms and disease. The flea is a carrier of tapeworm, and may act as an intermediate host for heartworm. The tick can cause dermatitis and anemia in your dog, and may also be a carrier of Rocky Mountain spotted fever and canine babesiasis, a blood infection.

## External Parasites

The dog that is groomed regularly and provided with clean sleeping quarters should not be troubled by fleas, ticks, or lice. If the dog should become infested with any of these parasites, he should be treated with medicated dip bath or the new oral medications that are presently available.

## Mange

There are two types of mange, sarcoptic and follicular, both of which are caused by a parasite. The former is by far the more common, and results in an intense irritation, causing violent scratching. Close examination will reveal small red spots which become filled with pus. This is a highly contagious condition, and any dog showing signs of the disease should be isolated. Consult your veterinarian for the proper treatment procedures. Follicular mange is very much harder to cure, but fortunately, it is much rarer and less contagious. This disease will manifest itself as bare patches appearing on the skin, which becomes thickened and leathery. A complete cure from this condition is only rarely effected.

## Eczema

This disease occurs most often in the summer months and affects the dog down the back, especially just above the root of the tail. It should not be confused with mange, as it is not caused by a parasite. One of the principle causes of eczema is improper nutrition, which makes the dog susceptible to disease. Hot, humid weather predisposes the growth of bacteria, which can invade a susceptible dog and thereby cause skin irritations and lesions. It is imperative that the dog gets relief from the itching that is symptomatic of the disease as this self-mutilation by scratching will only help to spread the inflammation. Antibiotics may be necessary if a bacterial infection is, indeed, present. The dog must be thoroughly ridded of fleas to avoid any recurrance of the scratching that can spread the disease.

Moist eczema, commonly referred to as "hot spots," is a rapidly appearing skin disease that produces a moist infection. Spots appear very suddenly and may spread rapidly in a few hours, infecting several parts of the body. These lesions are generally bacterially infected and are extremely itchy, which will cause the dog to scratch frantically and further damage the afflicted areas. Vomiting, fever and an enlargement of the lymph nodes may occur. The infected areas must be clipped to the skin and thoroughly cleaned. Your veterinarian will prescribe an anti-inflammatory drug and antibiotics, as well as a soothing emollient to relieve itching.

## EYES, EARS, TEETH AND NAILS

If your dog is to remain in good health, you must be aware of the need for periodic "examinations" in which you routinely inspect him for unusual signs of irritation or infection. In most cases, the tell-tale warning signals are any unusual swelling, discharge or redness that may appear, especially after an injury.

The eyes, because of their sensitivity, are prone to injury and infection. Dogs that spend a great deal of time outdoors in heavily wooded areas may return from an exercise excursion with watery eyes, the result of brambles and high weeds scratching them. The eyes may also be irritated by dirt and other foreign matter.

Should your dog's eyes appear red and watery, a mild solution can be mixed at home for a soothing washing. Your veterinarian will be able to tell you what percentage of boric acid, salt, or other medicinal compound to mix with water.

You must monitor your dog's eyes after such a solution is administered; if the irritation persists, or if there is a significant discharge, immediate veterinary attention is warranted.

Your dog's ears, like his eyes, are extremely sensitive and can also be prone to infection, should wax and/or dirt be allowed to build up. Ear irritants may be present in the form of mites, soap or water, or foreign par-

The Elizabethan collar is designed to keep your dog from scratching the area about his head and ears when a wound or sutures there advise against scratching. While they can be purchased ready-made, they can also be easily made at home from a piece of cardboard box. Be sure the hole is large enough so that it does not constrict the dog's breathing or swallowing.

ticles which the dog has come into contact with while romping through a wooded area. If your dog's ears are bothering him, you will know it—he will scratch and paw them, shake his head, and the ears will show a foulsmelling dark secretion. This pasty secretion usually signals the onset of *otorrhea*, or ear canker, and at this stage proper veterinary care is essential if the dog's hearing is not to be permanently impaired. In the advanced stages of ear canker, tissue builds up within the ear, and the ear canal becomes blocked off, thus eliminating the hearing abilities of that ear.

If this is to be prevented, you should wash your dog's ears as they require it, with a very dilute solution of hydrogen peroxide and water, or an antibacterial ointment, as your vet suggests. In any case, the ears, because of their delicacy, are to be washed gently, with a soft cloth or cotton.

The good health of your pet's teeth can be maintained by his regular use of a chew product such as Nylabone® or Nylaball®, which serves to clean the teeth of tartar accumulation and massage and stimulate the gums. With puppies, a chew product helps to relieve the discomfort of the teething stage, and of course prevents the pup's chewing of your furniture and slippers!

A periodic inspection of your dog's mouth will alert you to any problem he might have that would require a trip to the veterinarian's office. Any signs of tooth or gum sensitivity, redness or swelling, signal the need for professional treatment. Also, it is best to have your pet's teeth scraped once or twice a year, at the time that he goes to the vet's for his general physical check-up. This simple procedure removes any excess tartar that

Badly decayed teeth can cause abscesses of mouth tissues and gums, and even bone deterioration in extreme cases. Pain caused by such a condition can discourage your dog from eating even though he is hungry, resulting in possible malnutrition or even starvation. Your vet should be consulted if any listlessness or change in eating habits is noticed.

Dog nail clippers are designed to trim nails quickly and easily with a minimum of scuffling between you and your dog. While other general purpose instruments can be used, there is a greater chance with these of cutting too far down on the nail and hitting the vein, resulting in a painful experience for your dog.

has accumulated on his teeth that could cause degeneration of tooth enamel, if left to build up.

If you live in a city and walk your dog regularly on pavement, chances are that his nails are kept trimmed from the "wear and tear" they receive from the sidewalks. However, if your dog gets all of his exercise in your yard, or if his nails simply grow rather quickly, it will occasionally be necessary for you to clip his nails. It is best for you to have your veterinarian show you the proper way to perform the nail clipping at first. Special care must always be taken to avoid cutting too far and reaching the "quick." If you cut into the quick of the nail, it will bleed, so it is easy to see why an expert must show you the proper procedure. A nail clipper designed especially for dogs can be purchased at any pet shop.

## CARE OF THE AGED DOG

With the increased knowledge and care available, there is no reason why your dog should not live to a good old age. As the years go by he may need a little additional care. Remember that an excessively fat dog is not healthy, particularly as he grows older, so limit the older dog's food accordingly. He needs exercise as much as ever, although his heart cannot bear the strain of sudden and violent exertion. Failing eyesight or hearing means lessened awareness of dangers, so you must protect him more than ever.

Should you decide at this time to get a puppy, to avoid being without a dog when your old friend is no longer with you, be very careful how you introduce the puppy. He naturally will be playful and will expect the older dog to respond to his advances. Sometimes the old dog will get a new lease on life from a new puppy, but he may be consumed with jealousy. Do not give the newcomer the attention that formerly was exclusively the older dog's. Feed them apart, and show your old friend that you still love him the most; the puppy, not being accustomed to individual attention, will not mind sharing your love.

## TATTOOING

Tattooing is an increasingly popular method of identifying your dog that has met with growing success in assuring the safe return of lost or stolen dogs. Several registries exist that will record a dog's tattoo number along with his owner's name, address and telephone number. Two types of tattoo numbers can be assigned. In the case of mixed breed dogs, the owner's social security number is generally used; in the case of pedigreed dogs, the dog's AKC registration number is used. These two numbers are the most common means of identification. The groin or inside of the ear is the usual spot for the tattoo mark, though cases have been cited in which a dog's ear was cut off to eliminate the possibility of catching the dognappers.

For a minor fee, your veterinarian can do the simple, painless job that may insure the return of a beloved pet or show dog. Such return would be reward enough for the few minutes it takes to have this simple procedure done. Since a puppy grows very rapidly, it is best not to have him tattooed until he is at least four months old to avoid any possible smearing of the tattoo ink. There is almost no danger of infection if the job is done properly and exhibitors run no risk of having the show dog's career impaired by the tattoo mark since the AKC has ruled that no judge may disqualify or penalize a dog because of a tattoo.

Your local kennel club will be able to supply the name of a registry in your area.

# 9. DOG SHOW COMPETITION

There is no greater pleasure for the owner than showing a beautiful dog perfectly groomed and trained for the show ring. Whether he wins or not, it is gratifying to show a dog in superb condition, one that is a credit to your training and care. A great deal of preparation, both for you and your dog, is needed before the day that you do any serious winning. Showing is not as easy as it looks, even if you have a magnificent dog. He must be presented to the judge so that all of his good points are shown to advantage. This requires practice in gaiting, daily grooming from puppyhood, and the proper diet to make him sound in body.

When you buy your puppy you probably will think he is the best in the country and possibly in the world, but before you enter the highly competitive world of dog shows, get an unbiased expert opinion. Visit a few dog shows as a spectator and make mental notes of what is required of the handlers and dogs. Watch how the experienced handlers manage their dogs to bring out their best points.

## HOW TO SELECT A SHOW DOG

If you are planning to show your dog, it is best not to buy a puppy any younger than four or six months of age. Since it is difficult at best to predict what a puppy will look like at maturity, you cannot rely wholly on its appearance while it is only six or eight weeks old. By doing a certain amount of homework before purchasing your show dog, you can be assured to an extent that you will end up with a show quality dog that will hold its own in the show rings. Before going out to buy, read some good books on your breed. Consult a reputable book of standards for the breed to get an idea of what the dog should look like as an adult. Remember that no individual dog ever completely achieves the standard, but knowing the important conformational points of the breed will help to illustrate what you are aiming for in your show dog. Attending dog shows and talking with veterans who have been in the dog game for a while will give you valuable information to use when choosing your own show prospect.

One of the best assurances you can get in a field where there are no real guarantees is to search out well-known breeders who are known to have successfully bred show winners through several generations. Ask to look at the pedigree of any puppy you are considering buying, noting whether there are numerous top-quality dogs in the ancestry. Have the sire and

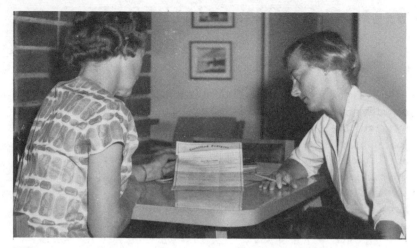

When you purchase your puppy, the breeder can supply you with a pedigree for him. A puppy of champion bloodlines is often of superior quality.

dam of the litter you are interested in been bred before, and if so, what was the overall quality of their previous offspring? If they have produced consistently good dogs through several of the same pairings, your chances of getting a good specimen are fairly high. If the stud or bitch, or both, are unproven in previous litters, the probability of attaining top quality in the puppies is less likely.

In general, the rule of thumb to follow is to go by the expertise of the breeder. A reputable breeder will sell you the best dog possible if you make it clear to him that the dog will definitely be used for a show career. The show contender you purchase not only represents you as its owner, but also reflects the quality of the kennel of the breeder. The reputation of both exhibitor and breeder is made by the quality of the dogs they present, so careful selection of a show dog is essential to all involved.

## TYPES OF DOG SHOWS

There are various types of dog shows. The American Kennel Club sanctioned matches are shows at which purebred dogs may compete, but not for championship points. These are excellent for you to enter to accustom you and your dog to showing. If your dog places in a few match shows, then you might seriously consider entering the big-time shows. An American Kennel Club all-breed show is one at which purebred dogs compete for championship points. An American Kennel Club specialty show is for one breed only. It may be held in conjunction with an all-breed show (by designating the classes at that show as its specialty show) or it may be held entirely apart. Obedience trials are different in that in them the dog is judged according to his obedience and ability to perform, not by his conformation to the breed standard.

There are two types of championship conformation shows: *benched* and *unbenched.* At a benched show your dog must be on his appointed bench during the advertised hours of the show's duration. He may be removed from the bench only to be taken to the exercise pen or to be groomed (an hour before the showing) in an area designated for handlers to set up their crates and grooming tables. At an unbenched show your car may serve as a bench for your dog.

To become a champion your dog must win fifteen points in competition with other dogs; a portion of the fifteen points must be awarded as major point wins (three to five points) under different judges.

This scene from a large indoor show captures the exciting moment when the group winners go before the judge for the Best In Show competition.

## HOW TO ENTER

If your dog is purebred and registered with the AKC—or eligible for registration—you may enter him in the appropriate show class for which his age, sex, and previous show record qualify him. You will find coming shows listed in the different dog magazines or at your petshop. Write to the secretary of the show, asking for the premium list. When you receive the entry form, fill it in carefully and send it back with the required entry fee. Then, before the show, you should receive your exhibitor's pass, which will admit you and your dog to the show. Here are the five official show classes:

*PUPPY CLASS:* Open to dogs at least six months and not more than twelve months of age. Limited to dogs whelped in the United States and Canada.

*NOVICE CLASS:* Open to dogs six months of age or older that have never won a first prize in any class other than puppy class, and less than three first prizes in the novice class itself. Limited to dogs whelped in the United States or Canada.

*BRED BY EXHIBITOR CLASS:* Open to all dogs, except cham-

To transport your dog long distances, crates should be used that have been made especially for that purpose. They are designed to give your dog optimum ventilation and comfort, while still assuring his maximum safety and protection.

Your pet store carries a large number of pet feeding and watering bowls, in sizes suitable for any size dog. While at a show, be sure to supply your dog with a light meal and some fresh water to keep him comfortable.

pions, six months of age or over which are exhibited by the same person, or his immediate family, or kennel that was the recognized breeder on the records of the American Kennel Club.

*AMERICAN-BRED CLASS:* Open to dogs that are not champions, six months of age or over, whelped in the United states after a mating which took place in the United States.

*OPEN CLASS:* Open to dogs six months of age or over, with no exceptions.

In addition there are local classes, the Specials Only class, and brace and team entries.

For full information on dog shows, read the book *How to Show Your Own Dog,* by Virginia Tuck Nichols. (T.F.H.)

### JUNIOR SHOWMANSHIP

If you have considered that you and your dog are going to go the show route, you might consider having your youngster show the dog in the ring. If your child has an especially good relationship with his pet, or if he has trained the dog himself, as many children do, then Junior Showmanship might be a good learning experience.

Junior Showmanship is competition among children of different age groups, handling dogs owned by their immediate families. The age divisions are: Novice A, for 10 to 12 year olds; Novice B, for those boys and girls from 13 to 16 (entrants in these two classes must have one or no prior Junior Showmanship wins); Open A for those 10 to 12 years of age; Open B for those 13 to 16 (these entrants must have earned two or more Junior Showmanship awards).

Children involved in JS have the wonderful opportunity to feel a sense of achievement and victory, should they walk away with the ribbons after a show. Even still, winning is not the most important factor here: the pride and responsibility the youngster feels at having reached the ring is surely worth the effort and discipline required to enter showmanship competition.

For more information on JS, and to obtain a rules and regulations booklet, you can contact the American Kennel Club in New York.

## ADVANCED PREPARATION

Before you go to a show your dog should be trained to gait at a trot beside you, with head up and in a straight line. In the ring you will have to gait your dog around the edge with other dogs and then individually up and down the center runner. In addition the dog must stand for ex-

If yours is intended to be a show dog, you will want to be prepared with all the tools and equipment necessary for the meticulous grooming of a show dog. Several different types of combs, brushes, clippers and coat grooming products can be obtained from the local pet store.

Be sure to take along a comfortable carrier for your dog if he is to be confined, or benched, during the show's duration.

amination by the judge, who will look at him closely and feel his head and body structure. He should be taught to stand squarely, hind feet slightly back, head up on the alert. Showing requires practice training sessions in advance. Get a friend to act as judge and set the dog up and "show" him a few minutes every day.

Sometime before the show, give your dog a bath so he will look his best. Get together all the things you will need to take to the show. You will want to take a water dish and a bottle of water for your dog (so he won't be affected by a change in drinking water). Take your show lead, bench chain (if it is a benched show), combs and brush, and the identification ticket sent by the show superintendent, noting the time you must be there and the place where the show will be held, as well as the time of judging.

**THE DAY OF THE SHOW**

Don't feed your dog the morning of the show, or give him at most a light meal. He will be more comfortable in the car on the way, and will show more enthusiastically. When you arrive at the show grounds, find out where he is to be benched and settle him there. Your bench or stall

Conformation to the ideal standard for the breed will be recognized in show dogs by the awarding of ribbons and trophies. Dog show entrants can win on several different levels, with the most significant and exciting award being Best In Show honors.

number is on your identification ticket, and the breed name will be on placards fastened to the ends of the row of benches. Once you have your dog securely fastened to his stall by a bench chain (use a bench crate instead of a chain if you prefer), locate the ring where your dog will be judged (the number and time of showing will be on the program of judging which came with your ticket). After this you may want to take your dog to the exercise ring to relieve himself, and give him a small drink of water. Your dog will have been groomed before the show, but give him a final brushing just before going into the show ring. When your breed judging is called, it is your responsibility to be at the ringside ready to go in. The steward will give you an armband which has on it the number of your dog.

Then, as you step into the ring, try to keep your knees from knocking! Concentrate on your dog and before you realize it you'll be out again, perhaps back with the winners of each class for more judging and finally, with luck, it will be over and you'll have a ribbon and trophy—and, of course, the most wonderful dog in the world!

# 10. BUILDING A KENNEL AND EXERCISE RUNS

## DRAWING UP PLANS

Whether you have one dog or many, the time may come when you decide that an outdoor kennel and runs will best satisfy your dog's exercise and housing needs. Properly built and maintained, a kennel offers your dog the comfort of dry living quarters, adequate ventilation and sunlight, and the availability of regular exercise.

Before you begin to draw up plans for kennel construction, check with your town's municipal offices to see if a building permit is required and which, if any, regulations of the building code you must adhere to. The permit, if required, must be obtained before any construction is begun. Building a kennel is not a small undertaking, so pre-planning on all fronts will prevent unexpected snags from cropping up, causing time delays and inconveniences.

One of the first decisions to make concerns the choice between building the kennel yourself as a sort of family project, or hiring a general contractor to do the work. If you decide on the latter, details of financing, building plans and blueprints to suit your needs should be worked out before contractual agreements are signed. For the plans on actual construction, including a concrete foundation, framework and overall structure, you should consult an architect who will, for a fee, draw up a set of blueprints for you or a contractor to follow. Have the architect see your land, and detail clearly to him each specific feature you want designed into the building. In this way you will enable him to set down a precise set of blueprints, meeting your specifications.

## LAND AND SPACE REQUIREMENTS

To build an average size kennel, you must have a significant parcel of land to set aside for this purpose. The location of the building site should provide adequate sunlight and shade for warmth and coolness throughout the seasons. The soil should be of a high gravel content as a gravel soil provides good drainage. By comparison, a sandy soil, though its surface dries quickly, retains dampness and residual dirt just beneath the surface. It is also a favorite breeding place of fleas and similar pests.

Drainage is a prime consideration, not only to let natural ground water run off, but also to let the water drain off from the frequent hosings a kennel must be given to ensure cleanliness and prevent growth of disease-producing germs. A kennel should be trenched for drainage much the way a soldier trenches around his tent. One continuous drainage ditch approximately eight inches wide should be dug around all sides of the kennel, no further than a foot away from the kennel walls. It should be dug to a depth of four inches to start with, sloping an additional inch for every three yards of land. With ditches extending from at least two front corners of the building down to this surrounding ditch, water will run away from the building to the lowest point of land, preventing moisture build-up or preventing the water to lay near the kennel building itself. The drainage system can be sophisticated further, the ditch tiled, for instance, and eventually connecting with or running to a storm drain. Whatever else is devised, drainage should definitely figure into your building plans.

## BUILDING MATERIALS

The building materials you use are of great importance. Not only must they be of good quality but they must be of a type that will protect the dog from the elements. For example, sheet metal, a conductor of both heat and cold, should never be used for the outside walls or ceilings. It becomes extremely hot in the sun and will retain heat in the kennel, making a potentially dangerous and certainly uncomfortable situation for the dogs. Outside walls should ideally be constructed from lumber, bricks or cinder blocks. The walls must be insulated with a substance that will serve equally well in all seasons, protecting your dogs from the heat and the cold.

Interior walls can be constructed of wood, plywood or plaster board. Plywood has the advantage of being extremely durable; however, plywood is quite expensive and can give way to splintering should the dogs scratch at it. Plaster board, also commonly known as sheet rock, is inexpensive and relatively durable. Plaster board does not, however, stand up well to moisture, but more than compensates for this drawback by being very resistant to insect and rodent infestation.

The above plans detail the probable steps involved in the construction of a rather large kennel, suited for up to a dozen dogs. At first, most dog owners have only one or two dogs that they want to provide for. If this is the case, a large dog house, modified somewhat, will aptly serve until such time that a larger kennel is needed.

## THE SINGLE DOG HOUSE

While a dog will be contented with less living space than his master is accustomed to, his own house should be large enough to allow for free space around and above him when he stands up in the enclosure. The size of the dog house depends, of course, on the size of the dog.

Using materials purchased from any lumber store, you can build a dog house yourself. When constructing the house, take care to finish it off well, leaving no nails or wood splinters protruding from the wood which could injure the dog.

If you wish to move your pet into a new, ready-to-go home, finished dog houses can be purchased in varying styles and price ranges. Your pet shop may have some houses in stock; if not, the owner can probably suggest an outlet where one would be available. The yellow pages of your phone directory may also be useful in locating an establishment that carries dog houses, either constructed or in kits. Some of the latest styles available are quite pleasing to the eye, such as the house constructed out of unstripped logs, designed to give your dog his own little log cabin! If you check various outlets you will find that dog houses range in design from the simple to the elaborate.

## CARE OF THE DOG HOUSE

To prevent dampness and to retain heat in the dog house, it should not be placed directly on the ground, but elevated at least several inches. A 2″ x 4″ beam placed under two opposing sides of the house, with the 4″ side lying flat on the ground, should allow for proper ventilation beneath the structure. However, in winter months you will want to close off this space to prevent drafts. In this case, boards can easily and quickly be nailed between the 2″ x 4″'s already in place to cover the exposed openings. Keeping the dog house a proper distance from the ground also serves to prevent the possibility of water damage, which will cause the wood to warp and eventually decay. Infestation of the wood by insects can be prevented by keeping the primary wood of the house from contact with the dirt below.

Whether kept in the yard or in the garage, the single dog house has the advantage of being able to be moved from spot to spot. Moving the dog house will be necessary occasionally for such reasons as cleaning, moving into or out of direct sunlight or shade, etc. This is an advantage when you consider that in the cold winter months your dog may very much appreciate having his house placed in direct sunlight! In cold weather the dog house can be positioned with the entranceway facing east or south, to receive full sunlight.

If a shifting of position is all that is needed, a strong friend or two should be able to help relocate the house. However, if the move is for a considerable distance and your dog house is quite heavy, a moving dolly may be necessary.

1

2

3

(1) All three colors of Labrador can occur in the same litter, but a litter can also be composed solely of blacks and chocolates. (2) To participate either in conformation shows or field trials, your Lab must know basic obedience commands to succeed. (3) The field dog must satisfy his chewing needs in acceptable ways so he won't be tempted to do so when retrieving game. This Lab chews on a flavor impregnated nylon bone, the safest kind. (4) Dark eyes and noses are preferred in all colors of Lab, but because of the less predictable outcome in breeding for chocolate, the dark points are more difficult to attain.

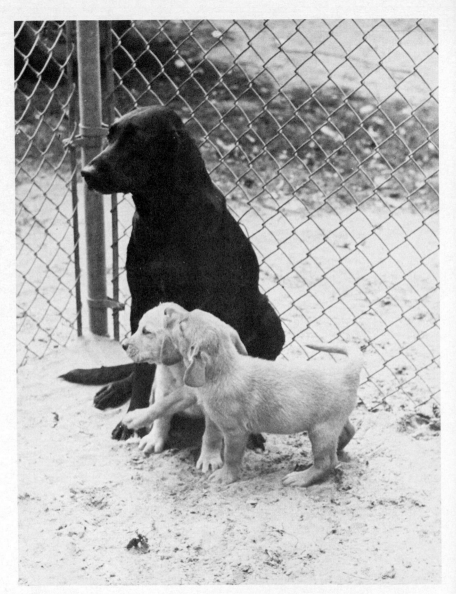

Three colors are recognized in the Labrador Retriever: black, yellow and chocolate. Black parents can give birth to all of these, but before serious color breeding is considered, a basic grounding in genetics is necessary.

# 11. COLOR BREEDING

Three solid colors are recognized for the Labrador. These are black, yellow and chocolate. Records of long standing indicate that these same coat colors have always existed for the Lab, and in fact were common even long before careful breeding records were kept. Blacks, however, were long the most favored color, believed to be much hardier and adept at their retrieving instincts than members of the breed bearing the other two colors. Competition in today's field and obedience trials have proven this belief to be false, with dogs of all three colors being equally proficient.

Black coats in Labradors are a dominant color. From a genetic point of view, matings between black-coated Labs can produce puppies with three different possible genetic structures. If the parents in one mating are both pure for black, that is carry only dominant black genes, then all of the puppies will be both black in color and have a genetic makeup pure for black. If one parent in a mating is pure for black and the other appears black but carries a recessive yellow gene, half of the puppies in the resulting litter will be black in color and have the genetic makeup of the parent that is pure for black. The other half of the litter will be black in color but will have the genetic makeup of the other parent who carries a recessive yellow gene. If two puppies of this litter having the genetic structure of the parent carrying the recessive yellow were mated in adulthood they would produce a litter in which one quarter of the pups were pure for black; one quarter were the product of the pairing of the two recessives and were pure for yellow; and one half had the same genetic structure of both parents, being black in color and each carrying a recessive yellow gene. Dogs that carry a dominant and a recessive gene are referred to as hybrids. Mating between a dog that is pure for black and one that is pure for yellow will produce all hybrid puppies, that is all the offspring will be black in color but will all carry the recessive gene for yellow.

Yellow coat color can occur only when two recessive genes are paired. So, if two dogs are mated that are both pure for yellow, all the resulting puppies will be yellow in color and have the genetic makeup of both parents; that is, they will carry only paired recessive genes for yellow. In the case of the hybrid black, it is possible for one individual in a mating between phenotypical (refers to appearance of individual dogs) black dogs to pass on the recessive yellow genes through generations of black dogs, with a yellow pup finally occuring only when a hybrid parent is mated to another black hybrid parent. Even though nowhere in the pedigrees of

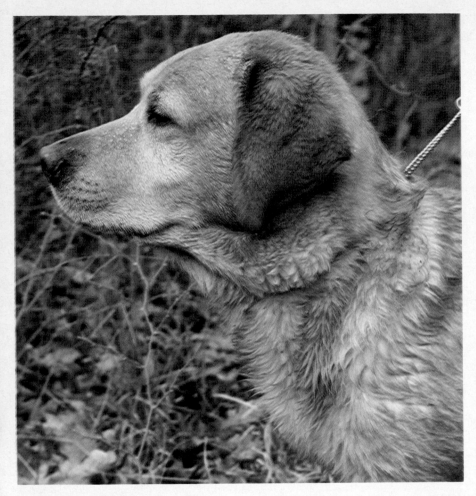

In yellow Labs the color may vary from fox-red to light cream. The coat should, however, be of the same even shading throughout, except for the ears, which may be darker, and underparts and beneath the tail where shadings may also occur.

Breeding blacks to chocolates, such as those pictured in (1) has proven to yield the highest percentage of appropriately colored chocolates. (2) Breeders have found that breeding a black to a chocolate capable of producing blacks results in puppies that have the desirable eyes and points.

1    2

(1) Breeding pedigreed dogs should always be accompanied by the presence of at least one handler, and for larger dogs, even two or three. Here, a bitch and her intended stud approach each other. Time should be allowed for courting activity. This "getting to know" period facilitates the actual mating, allowing the dogs to feel comfortable with each other. (2) The bitch that has been mated at the proper time in her cycle will "stand" for the stud, cocking her tail to one side to facilitate his entry.

1

2

3

(3) In cases where the dogs may separate before a successful mating, a handler may hold them together. (4) After the tie has taken place, the two are not able to separate for up to 30 minutes. During this time, the male will turn, swinging one hind leg over the female's rear haunches so that both dogs are standing with all four feet on the ground. (5) After the turn, the dogs may rest back to back or side by side.

5

4

(1) The Labrador is a calm yet active dog. In the case of a field dog especially, the high energy level must be properly channeled when he is not exercising his hunting instincts. (2) Enforcing house rules with your Lab not only makes him easier to live with, but if he is a field dog helps reinforce the discipline necessary to retrieving activities. (3) This fine trio of yellow exhibits the attentiveness that makes them one of the most popular hunting dogs.

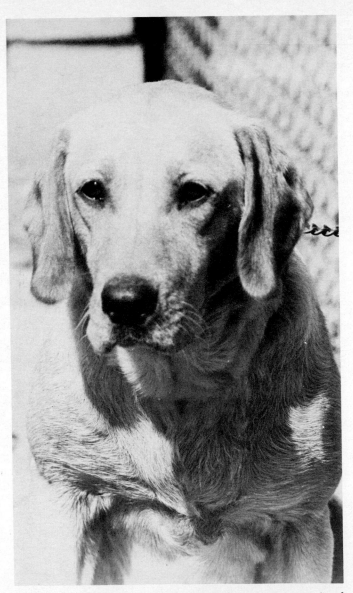

The yellow color in a Labrador Retriever is the result of pairing between two recessive genes. While black parents may produce yellow offspring, yellows bred to yellows will always produce yellows.

past lineages for several hundred generations can a yellow parent be found.

The first recognized yellow, Ben of Hyde, was whelped in England in 1899. He had been bred from two black parents descended from those first Labs that reached England via the cod ships from Newfoundland. Though the bitches to whom he was bred were all blacks, Ben sired many yellows among his offspring. His yellow sister Juno, however, failed to produce any yellows when she was bred to black dogs.

After World War I, kennels began to specialize in breeding yellows. Proliferation of yellow-coated Labs was encouraged about this time to guarantee support of their class at shows against a prejudice for blacks. In order to compete with the established, classic, black Labs, much careful breeding was necessary, with a thorough-going knowledge of lineage, where it was available, required of breeders.

Chocolate Labradors have been known in the breed as long as the other colors. It is not inherited as a simple recessive, and breeders have not yet established a definite breeding pattern for producing consistently even-colored chocolate dogs of the same color intensity and possessing the dark points. Chocolates bred to chocolates will not invariably produce chocolate pups as in the case of the recessive yellow parents. In one litter of record where two chocolates were bred together, five offspring were yellow and five were chocolate. All of the yellows in this litter had light eyes, but evidently none of the chocolates had them.

Light eyes have been a problem in the breeding of chocolates. It is felt by many breeders that it is possible to get the dark points only when chocolates are bred to blacks. Some geneticists believe that the chocolate color is produced through a modifying action by genes of partial dominance which dilute or blend with the color produced by genes for other colors. Some breeders feel that to get dark eyes in chocolates, chocolate colored dogs having black parents must be bred to black dogs known to be producers of chocolate-coated dogs.